**1st EDITION**

# Perspectives on Diseases and Disorders

## Cystic Fibrosis

Jacqueline Langwith
*Book Editor*

Detroit • New York • San Francisco • New Haven, Conn • Waterville, Maine • London

Christine Nasso, *Publisher*
Elizabeth Des Chenes, *Managing Editor*

© 2009 Greenhaven Press, a part of Gale, Cengage Learning

Articles in Greenhaven Press anthologies are often edited for length to meet page requirements. In addition, original titles of these works are changed to clearly present the main thesis and to explicitly indicate the author's opinion. Every effort is made to ensure that Greenhaven Press accurately reflects the original intent of the authors. Every effort has been made to trace the owners of copyrighted material.

Cover image Custom Medical Stock Photo, Inc. Reproduced by permission.

LIBRARY OF CONGRESS CATALOGING-IN-PUBLICATION DATA

Cystic fibrosis / Jacqueline Langwith, book editor.
   p. cm. — (Perspectives on diseases and disorders)
  Includes bibliographical references and index.
  ISBN 978-0-7377-4245-9 (hardcover)
  1. Cystic fibrosis. I. Langwith, Jacqueline.
  RC858.C95C933 2009
  616.3'7—dc22
                                             2008031769

Printed in the United States of America
1 2 3 4 5 6 7 12 11 10 09 08

# CONTENTS

# INTRODUCTION

Margaret is thirty-five years old and the mother of three children ranging in age from two to ten years old. Margaret and her family live in a small midwestern town. They have a dog named Dexter, and the whole family loves watching hockey. Margaret sounds like a perfectly typical midwestern mom. However, Margaret is far from typical. She has a disease that used to kill children well before they ever reached adulthood. Now that medical advances are enabling cystic fibrosis (CF) sufferers to live into their twenties and thirties, Margaret and many other women with CF are having children. However, the demands of pregnancy and motherhood are very difficult for women with cystic fibrosis. Some women decide not to have children for health reasons and because they do not believe it is fair to the child. However, many women, like Margaret, have a strong desire to conceive their own child and to be mothers, in spite of their disease.

Cystic fibrosis used to be a childhood disease, but throughout the twentieth century the survival rate for cystic fibrosis patients continually increased. In the 1900s babies born with the affliction typically lived only a few months. By the 1950s most children born with CF died before they even went to elementary school. From the 1950s onward, as antibiotic use became more widespread, CF patients gained more and more ground. In the 1960s they started living beyond their teens. In 1985 the median predicted survival age for cystic fibrosis patients reached twenty-five years. CF was no longer a disease for children only. Cystic fibrosis patients were growing up, graduating from high school, going to college, and getting married.

In 2007 the life expectancy for people with cystic fibrosis was thirty-seven years.

As women with cystic fibrosis reached child-bearing age, many of them desired to have children. The disease does not prevent women from becoming pregnant. However, it does affect men. In men with CF, the vas deferens, which is the tube that carries sperm, becomes blocked with mucus. Sperm are still made, but they are not released during ejaculation. As a result men with CF are infertile. In women with CF, mucus may build up in the reproductive tract and make fertilization of the egg more difficult than normal, but not impossible. In fact, most women with CF can become pregnant. The first documented case of a CF woman giving birth occurred in 1960. The baby was healthy, but tragically, the woman died six weeks later.

Pregnancy is risky for women with CF, and motherhood is demanding. Some of them decide to forgo pregnancy, while others resolve to give birth even with the associated risks. During pregnancy a woman's heart has to work harder. Her metabolism speeds up, and her nutritional requirements increase. CF makes it harder for the heart to get oxygen and harder for the digestive tract to absorb nutrients. Pregnant CF women are at risk of being poorly nourished and having poorly nourished babies. Beth, a young woman with CF, discusses her reasons for adopting a baby rather than trying to give birth:

> For me, the idea of being pregnant and all the health risks that come along with pregnancy did not seem like the healthiest way to become a parent. After all, my goal was to be a parent, not to experience pregnancy. I was assured that my decision to adopt rather than become pregnant was an extremely wise decision after my first day of parenthood. If I had gone through a pregnancy, I strongly suspect I would have gotten deathly ill when it came time to care for my baby.

A view of a cystic fibrotic bronchiole blocked with mucus is shown. Mucus also prevents secretion of digestive enzymes into the intestine. (© 2008/ **Jupiterimages**)

Tricia, another woman with cystic fibrosis, found out she was pregnant when she went in for a pre–lung-transplant doctor's appointment. She was told that she and her baby each had a 50 percent chance of survival. Tricia decided to go through with the pregnancy, which turned out to be very difficult. At one point, she was given a tracheostomy and put on a ventilator. Her health continued to decline so much that her doctors performed an emergency C-section: Baby Gwenyth was born three months prematurely. Immediately after giving birth, Tricia was placed in a medically induced coma for nine days. After being awakened, she slowly gained strength, and three months later Tricia received a double lung transplant. According to Tricia, Gwenyth was "worth the wait" and the sacrifice. Beth and Tricia offer differing viewpoints on the acceptability of the risks of pregnancy for women with cystic fibrosis.

Another debate about CF and motherhood centers on the impact on the child. Some people believe that people with CF should not have children, whether adopted or biological, because it is not fair to bring a child into the world who will undoubtedly lose a parent at a relatively young age. One mother, whose CF daughter unexpectedly got pregnant and gave birth to a child named Mayah Joell, believes women with CF should not become mothers. She describes the pain both her daughter and her granddaughter have gone through:

> I do not think that it is fair to have a child when you have a devastating fatal disease like cystic fibrosis. Mayah Joell is now five yrs, and her mom is dying. She is in the hospital with renal failure. . . . My daughter has had so much pain and gone through so much in her 26 yrs of life and it has been so hard for Mayah. She has a family who loves her more than life itself, but it kills me to see her so sad, so frustrated, so angry at the fact that her mom is sick.

Some CF patients defend their decision to become parents, believing that they can survive long enough to be good parents and arguing that all children face the risk of losing a parent. Beatrix Redemann, a new mother and a CF sufferer, says,

> It may be too simple to argue that every day many children lose one or both parents through war, accidents

and other mischief. These sort of deaths from injury are more or less unpredictable as opposed to the rather sure outcome of CF in which, statistically speaking, I have an increased chance of dying before the suggested average survival age for women in western countries. There might be people holding the opinion that my husband and I acted irresponsibly by taking this risk. However, from a current perspective, I should be able to survive long enough in relatively good shape to provide Ainu, [my daughter] with a capable mother during her growing years.

Whether to become a parent is not just a question for women with CF. Men with cystic fibrosis can adopt children. Additionally, advanced reproductive technologies are allowing men with CF to father children. Jeff Davis, who has CF, and his wife, Kim, have two children who were conceived using in vitro fertilization techniques. Doctors isolated Jeff's sperm and fertilized Kim's eggs in a petri dish. Jeff is always cognizant of the unpredictability of his health. He says, "Is it going to be a couple of years, or 20 years? Am I going to be there in their teenage years when they need me? Am I going to be there to guide them? Am I going to see [my daughter] get married? You have to take it all into consideration, but you can't let it rule your life."

The decision about whether to become a parent is just one of the many issues that people with cystic fibrosis must face, particularly as their life expectancy increases. In *Perspectives on Diseases and Disorders: Cystic Fibrosis*, many other issues surrounding the disease are introduced, discussed, and debated. The contributors provide information, insight, and personal stories in the following chapters: Understanding Cystic Fibrosis, Controversies About Cystic Fibrosis, and Personal Stories.

# CHAPTER 1

# Understanding Cystic Fibrosis

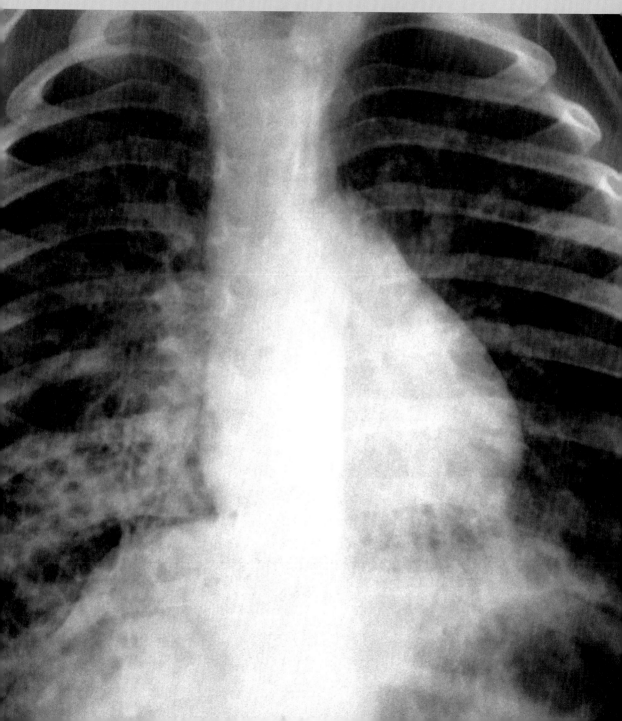

# An Overview of Cystic Fibrosis

## Richard Robinson and Tish Davidson

In the following article Richard Robinson and Tish Davidson discuss the causes, symptoms, and treatments of cystic fibrosis (CF), one of the most common inherited diseases in the United States. Cystic fibrosis affects the respiratory tract, the digestive tract, the sweat glands, and fertility. The most serious symptoms of the disease are related to the buildup of thick mucus in the lungs that promotes bacterial infections and makes breathing difficult. According to the authors, maintaining a healthy respiratory tract is critical for fighting the disease and living a normal life. This can be accomplished with proper nutrition, exercise, antibiotics, and various mucus-clearing treatments. Lung transplantation is also becoming more common for people with CF. Robinson and Davidson are nationally recognized medical writers.

Cystic fibrosis is caused by mutations (changes) in a gene that result in the production of a defective protein crucial to controlling water balance

Photo on facing page. A chest X-ray of a lung damaged by cystic fibrosis. (© Medical-on-Line/Alamy)

**SOURCE:** Richard Robinson and Tish Davidson, *The Gale Encyclopedia of Medicine.* Belmont, CA: Gale, 2007. Copyright © 2007 Gale. Reproduced by permission of Gale, a part of Cengage Learning.

in cells. This protein regulates the movement of sodium (Na+) and chloride (Cl-) ions in and out of cells. When the water balance in the cells is abnormal, the lungs, pancreas, and some other glands secrete thick mucus that makes breathing difficult and blocks the movement of digestive enzymes from the pancreas to the small intestine. Thick mucus also clogs sweat glands and salivary glands.

In 2007, CF affected approximately 30,000 people in the United States, and approximately 70,000 people worldwide. Around 1,000 new cases of CF are diagnosed each year, about 70% in children younger than three. CF primarily affects people of White Northern European descent (about 1 case in 3,200). Rates are much lower in non-white populations (about 1 case in 90,000 among Asians). In 2007, about 40% of Americans living with CF were adults. The average life expectancy for an individual with CF in 2007 was 37 years.

## Cystic Fibrosis Caused by Genetic Defect

Cystic fibrosis is a genetic disease, meaning it is inherited from one's parents. In 1989, a team of researchers located the gene that causes production of a defective version of an important protein called the CF transmembrane conductance regulator (CFTR). The defect in this gene leads to all the consequences of CF. There are over 1500 known defect variations in the CFTR gene that can cause CF. This appears to at least partially explain why there is variation in the severity of symptoms among individuals with CF. However, 70% of all people with a defective CFTR gene have the same defect, known as delta-F508.

Much as sentences are composed of strings of words, each made of letters, genes can be thought of as strings of chemical words, each made of chemical letters called nucleotides. Just as a sentence can be changed by rearranging its letters, genes can be mutated, or changed, by changes in the sequence of their nucleotide letters. The gene defects in CF are called point mutations, meaning that the gene is mutated only at one small spot along its length. In other words, the delta-F508 mutation is a loss of one "letter" out of thousands within the CFTR gene. As a result, the CFTR protein made from its blueprint is made incorrectly and cannot perform its function properly.

To have CF, a child must inherit two defective genes, one from each parent. People who inherit only one copy of the defective gene show no symptoms of CF. Approximately one in every 25 Americans of Northern European ancestry is a carrier of the mutated CF gene, while only one in 17,000 African Americans and one in 30,000 Asian Americans are carriers. Since carriers are symptom-free, very few people will know whether they are carriers unless there is a family history of the disease. Two white Americans with no family history of CF have about a one in 3,200 chance of having a child with CF.

> **FAST FACT**
>
> Cystic fibrosis is the most common fatal recessive genetic disorder among Caucasian people in the United States.

When both parents carry the defective CF gene, there is a one in two chance the child will inherit one defective gene and one good gene. This child will not have symptoms of cystic fibrosis but can pass the defective gene on to his or her children. There is a one in four chance the child will not inherit a defective gene from either parent, and also a one in four chance that the child will inherit two defective genes, one from each parent, and thus have CF.

## The Production of Thickened Mucus

The CFTR protein helps to regulate mucus production. Mucus is a complex mixture of salts, water, sugars, and proteins that cleanses, lubricates, and protects many passageways in the body, including those in the lungs and pancreas. The role of the CFTR protein is to allow chloride ions to exit the mucus-producing cells. When the chloride ions leave these cells, water follows, thinning the

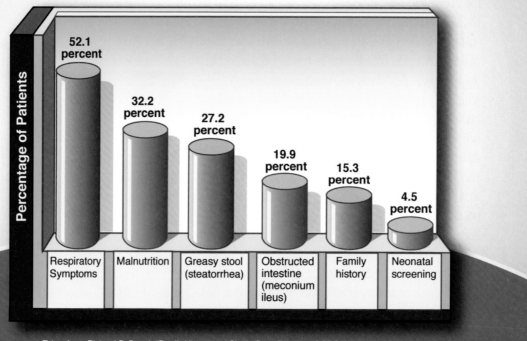

## Newly Diagnosed CF Patients: Symptoms, Family History, Screening

**Percentage of Patients**

- **52.1 percent** — Respiratory Symptoms
- **32.2 percent** — Malnutrition
- **27.2 percent** — Greasy stool (steatorrhea)
- **19.9 percent** — Obstructed intestine (meconium ileus)
- **15.3 percent** — Family history
- **4.5 percent** — Neonatal screening

Taken from: Richard B. Parad, "Family History and Single Gene Disorders," CDC Workgroup Meeting on Use of Family History Information in Pediatric Primary Care and Public Health, February 24–25, 2006.

mucus. In this way, the CFTR protein helps to keep mucus from becoming thick and sluggish, thus allowing the mucus to be moved steadily along the passageways to aid in cleansing.

In CF, the CFTR protein does not allow chloride ions to leave mucus-producing cells. With less chloride leaving, less water leaves, and the mucus becomes thick and sticky. It can no longer move freely through the passageways, so they become clogged. In the pancreas, clogged passageways prevent secretion of digestive enzymes into the intestine, causing serious impairment of digestion, especially of fat, that can lead to malnutrition. Mucus in the lungs may plug the airways, preventing good air exchange and, ultimately, leading to emphysema. The mucus is also a rich source of nutrients for bacteria, leading to frequent infections.

## CF Affects the Digestive System

The most severe effects of cystic fibrosis are seen in two body systems: the gastrointestinal (digestive) system, and the respiratory tract, from the nose to the lungs. CF also affects the sweat glands and male fertility. Symptoms develop gradually, with gastrointestinal symptoms often the first to appear.

Ten to fifteen percent of babies who inherit CF have meconium ileus at birth. Meconium is the first dark stool that a baby passes after birth; ileus is an obstruction of the digestive tract. The meconium of a newborn with meconium ileus is thickened and sticky, due to the presence of thickened mucus from the intestinal glands. Meconium ileus causes abdominal swelling and vomiting, and often requires surgery immediately after birth. Presence of meconium ileus is considered highly indicative of CF. Borderline cases may be misdiagnosed, however, and attributed instead to "milk allergy."

Other abdominal symptoms are caused by the inability of the pancreas to supply digestive enzymes to the intestine. During normal digestion, as food passes from the stomach into the small intestine, it is mixed with pancreatic secretions that help to break down the nutrients for absorption. While the intestines themselves also provide some digestive enzymes, the pancreas is the major source of enzymes for the digestion of all types of foods, especially fats and proteins.

In CF, thick mucus blocks the pancreatic duct, which is eventually closed off completely by scar tissue formation. This scar tissue or fibrosis gives CF its name. Scarring leads to a condition known as pancreatic insufficiency. Without pancreatic enzymes, large amounts of undigested food pass into the large intestine. Bacterial action on this rich food source can cause gas and abdominal swelling. The large amount of fat remaining in the feces makes it bulky, oily, and foul-smelling.

Because nutrients are only poorly digested and absorbed, the person with CF is often ravenously hungry, underweight, and shorter than expected for his or her age. When CF is not treated, a child may develop symptoms of malnutrition, including anemia, bloating, and, paradoxically, appetite loss.

Diabetes becomes increasingly likely as a person with CF ages. Scarring of the pancreas slowly destroys those pancreatic cells that produce insulin, causing type I, or insulin-dependent, diabetes.

Gallstones affect approximately 10% of adults with CF. Liver problems are less common, but can be caused by the buildup of fat within the liver. Complications of liver enlargement may include internal hemorrhaging, abdominal fluid (ascites), spleen enlargement, and liver failure.

Other gastrointestinal symptoms can include a prolapsed rectum, in which part of the rectal lining protrudes through the anus, intestinal obstruction, and rarely, intussusception, in which part of the intestinal tube telescopes into an adjoining piece of intestine, cutting off blood supply.

Somewhat fewer than 10% of people with CF are free of gastrointestinal symptoms. Most of these people do not have the delta-F508 mutation, but rather a different one, which presumably allows at least some of their CFTR proteins to function normally in the pancreas.

## CF's Effects on the Respiratory Tract

The respiratory tract includes the nose, the throat, the trachea (or windpipe), the bronchi (which branch off from the trachea within each lung), the smaller bronchioles, and the blind sacs called alveoli, in which gas exchange takes place between air and blood.

Swelling of the sinuses within the nose is common in people with CF. This usually shows up on x ray, and may aid the diagnosis of CF. However, this swelling, called pansinusitis, rarely causes problems and does not usually require treatment.

Nasal polyps, or growths, affect about one in five people with CF. These growths are not cancerous and do not require removal unless they become annoying. While nasal polyps appear in older people without CF, especially those with allergies, they are rare in children without CF.

The lungs are the site of the most life-threatening effects of CF. The production of a thick, sticky mucus increases the likelihood of infection, decreases the ability to protect against infection, causes inflammation and swelling, decreases the functional capacity of the lungs, and may lead to emphysema. People with CF live with chronic populations of bacteria in their lungs, and lung infection is the major cause of death for those with CF.

The bronchioles and bronchi normally produce a thin, clear mucus that traps foreign particles, including bacteria and viruses. Tiny hair-like projections on the surface of these passageways slowly sweep the mucus along, out of the lungs and up the trachea to the back of the throat where it may be swallowed or coughed up. This "mucociliary escalator" is one of the principal defenses against lung infection.

The thickened mucus of CF prevents easy movement out of the lungs, and increases the irritation and inflammation of lung tissue. This inflammation swells the passageways, partially closing them down, further hampering the movement of mucus. A person with CF is likely to cough more frequently and more vigorously as the lungs attempt to clean themselves out.

At the same time, infection becomes more likely since the mucus is a rich source of nutrients. Bronchitis, bronchiolitis, and pneumonia are frequent in CF. The most common infecting organisms are the bacteria *Staphylococcus aureus*, *Haemophilus influenzae*, and *Pseudomonas aeruginosa.* A small percentage of people with CF have infections caused by *Burkholderia cepacia,* a bacterium which is resistant to most current antibiotics. (*Burkholderia cepacia* was formerly known as *Pseudomonas cepacia.*) The fungus *Aspergillus fumigatus* may infect older children and adults.

The body's response to infection is to increase mucus production. However, white blood cells fighting the infection thicken the mucus even more as they break down and release their cell contents. These white blood cells also provoke more inflammation, continuing the downward spiral that marks untreated CF.

As mucus accumulates, it can plug the smaller passageways in the lungs, decreasing functional lung volume. Getting enough air can become difficult; tiredness, shortness of breath, and intolerance of exercise become more common. Because air passes obstructions more easily during inhalation than during exhalation, over time, air becomes trapped in the smallest chambers of the lungs, the alveoli. As millions of alveoli gradually expand, the chest takes on the enlarged, barrel-shaped appearance typical of emphysema.

For unknown reasons, recurrent respiratory infections lead to "digital clubbing," in which the last joint of the fingers and toes becomes slightly enlarged.

## CF Affects the Sweat Glands and Fertility

The CFTR protein helps to regulate the amount of salt in sweat. People with CF have sweat that is much saltier than normal, and measuring the saltiness of a person's sweat is the most important diagnostic test for CF. Parents may notice that their infants taste salty when they kiss them. Excess salt loss is not usually a problem except during prolonged exercise or heat. While older children and adults with CF compensate for this extra salt loss by eating more salty foods, infants and young children are in danger of suffering its effects (such as heat prostration), especially during summer. Heat prostration is marked by lethargy, weakness, and loss of appetite, and should be treated as an emergency condition.

Ninety-eight percent of men with CF are sterile, due to complete obstruction or absence of the vas deferens, the tube carrying sperm out of the testes. While boys and men with CF form normal sperm and have normal levels of sex hormones, sperm are unable to leave the testes, and fertilization is not possible. Most women with CF are fertile, although they often have more difficulty getting pregnant than women without CF. In both boys and girls, puberty is often delayed, most likely due to the effects of poor

Many women with cystic fibrosis can still become pregnant despite their disease. (© Chad Ehlers/Alamy)

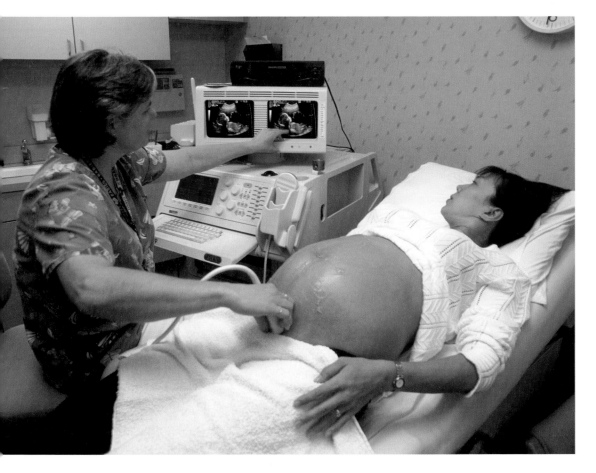

nutrition or chronic lung infection. Women with good lung health usually have no problems with pregnancy, while those with ongoing lung infection often do poorly.

## Diagnosing and Treating CF

The decision to test a child for cystic fibrosis may be triggered by concerns about recurring gastrointestinal or respiratory symptoms or salty sweat. A child born with meconium ileus will be tested before leaving the hospital. Families with a history of CF may wish to have all children tested, especially if there is a child who already has the disease. Some hospitals now require routine screening of newborns for CF. . . .

There is no cure for CF. Treatment has advanced considerably in the past several decades, increasing both the life span and the quality of life for most people affected by CF. Early diagnosis is important to prevent malnutrition and infection from weakening the young child. With proper management, many people with CF engage in the full range of school and sports activities.

People with CF usually require high-calorie diets and vitamin supplements. Height, weight, and growth of a person with CF are monitored regularly. Most people with CF need to take pancreatic enzymes to supplement or replace the inadequate secretions of the pancreas. Tablets containing pancreatic enzymes are taken with every meal; depending on the size of the tablet and the meal, as many as 20 tablets may be needed. Because of incomplete absorption even with pancreatic enzymes, a person with CF needs to take in about 30% more food than a person without CF. Low-fat diets are *not* recommended except in special circumstances, since fat is a source of both essential fatty acids and abundant calories. . . .

## Maintaining Respiratory Health Is Key

The key to maintaining respiratory health in a person with CF is regular monitoring and early treatment. Lung function tests are done frequently to track changes in functional lung volume and respiratory effort. Sputum samples are analyzed to determine the types of bacteria present in the lungs. Chest x rays are usually taken at least once a year. Lung scans, using a radioactive gas, can show closed off areas not seen on the x ray. Circulation in the lungs may be monitored by injection of a radioactive substance into the bloodstream.

People with CF live with chronic bacterial colonization; that is, their lungs are constantly host to several species of bacteria. Good general health, especially good nutrition, can keep the immune system healthy, which decreases the frequency with which these colonies begin an infection, or attack on the lung tissue. Exercise is another important way to maintain health, and people with CF are encouraged to maintain a program of regular exercise.

In addition, clearing mucus from the lungs helps to prevent infection; and mucus control is an important aspect of CF management. Postural drainage is used to allow gravity to aid the mucociliary escalator. For this technique, the person with CF lies on a tilted surface with head downward, alternately on the stomach, back, or side, depending on the section of lung to be drained. An assistant thumps the rib cage to help loosen the secretions. A device called a "flutter" offers another way to loosen secretions: it consists of a stainless steel ball in a tube. When a person exhales through it, the ball vibrates, sending vibrations back through the air in the lungs. Some special breathing techniques may also help clear the lungs.

Clearing the thick mucus from the lungs can also be accomplished by physiotherapy. Physiotherapy includes breathing exercises and percussion, the administration of blows to the back and chest to loosen the mucus. Some people with cystic fibrosis perform percussion on themselves but it is most effective when performed by someone else.

Several drugs are available to prevent the airways from becoming clogged with mucus. Bronchodilators and theophyllines open up the airways; steroids reduce inflammation; and mucolytics loosen secretions. Acetylcysteine (Mucomyst) has been used as a mucolytic for many years but is not prescribed frequently now, while DNase (Pulmozyme) is a newer product gaining in popularity. DNase breaks down the DNA from dead white blood cells and bacteria found in thick mucus.

People with CF may pick up bacteria from other CF patients. This is especially true of *Burkholderia cepacia*, which is not usually found in people without CF. While the ideal recommendation from a health standpoint might be to avoid contact with others who have CF, this is not usually practical since CF clinics are a major site of care, nor does it meet the psychological and social needs of many people with CF. At a minimum, CF centers recommend avoiding prolonged close contact between people with CF, and scrupulous hygiene, including frequent hand washing. Some CF clinics schedule appointments on different days for those with and without *B. cepacia* colonies.

## Treatment Options

Some doctors choose to prescribe antibiotics only during infection, while others prefer long-term antibiotic treatment against *S. aureus*. The choice of antibiotic depends on the particular organism or organisms found. Some antibiotics are given as aerosols directly into the lungs. Antibiotic treatment may be prolonged and aggressive.

Supplemental oxygen may be needed as lung disease progresses. Respiratory failure may develop, requiring temporary use of a ventilator to perform the work of breathing.

Lung transplantation has become increasingly common for people with CF, although the number of people who receive them is still much lower than those who want them. Transplantation is not a cure, however, and has been likened to trading one disease for another.

Long-term immunosuppression is required, increasing the likelihood of other types of infection. About 50% of adults and more than 80% of children who receive lung transplants live longer than two years. Liver transplants are also done for CF patients whose livers have been damaged by fibrosis.

Long-term use of ibuprofen has been shown to help some people with CF, presumably by reducing inflammation in the lungs. Close medical supervision is necessary, however, since the effective dose is high and not everyone benefits. Ibuprofen at the required doses interferes with kidney function, and together with aminoglycoside antibiotics, may cause kidney failure.

A number of experimental treatments are currently the subject of much research. Some evidence indicates that aminoglycoside antibiotics may help overcome the genetic defect in some CF mutations, allowing the protein to be made normally. While promising, these results would apply to only about 5% of those with CF.

Gene therapy is currently the most ambitious approach to curing CF. In this set of techniques, nondefective copies of the CFTR gene are delivered to affected cells, where they are taken up and used to create the CFTR protein. While elegant and simple in theory, gene therapy has met with a large number of difficulties in trials so far. Before gene therapy for cystic fibrosis is perfected, researchers must overcome several obstacles. The most important obstacle is the use of viruses as carriers for the normal genes. Some scientists contend that using viruses is simply too dangerous, especially for patients who already have a chronic debilitating disease. Furthermore, the genetic material of viruses is small compared to human genetic material and thus can mutate quickly. If a virus undergoes a mutation, a small chance exists that the mutation could result in an extremely dangerous disease. Clinical trials are underway to test new drugs and therapies for CF. . . .

## Natural Treatments

In homeopathic medicine, the symptoms of the disease would be addressed to enhance the quality of life for the person with cystic fibrosis. Treating the cause of CF, because of the genetic basis for the disease, is not possible. Naturopathic medicine seeks to treat the whole person, however, and in this approach might include:

- mucolytics to help thin mucus
- supplementation of pancreatic enzymes to assist in digestion
- respiratory symptoms can be addressed to open lung passages
- hydrotherapy techniques to help ease the respiratory symptoms and help the body eliminate
- immune enhancements can help prevent the development of secondary infections
- dietary enhancements and adjustments are used to treat digestive and nutritional problems

People with CF may lead relatively normal lives, with the control of symptoms. The possible effect of pregnancy on the health of a woman with CF requires careful consideration before beginning a family; as do issues of longevity, and their children's status as carriers. Although most men with CF are functionally sterile, new procedures for removing sperm from the testes are being tried, and may offer more men the chance to become fathers. In 2007, the average lifespan of a person with CF was 37 years.

# The Life Expectancy for Cystic Fibrosis Patients Has Increased

### Ben Whitford

In the following article Ben Whitford asserts that new treatments are giving cystic fibrosis patients an adulthood they never expected. Whitford says that when cystic fibrosis was first diagnosed in the 1930s, most patients died in infancy. But now, due to new treatments, many cystic fibrosis patients live well into adulthood and even have children of their own. According to Whitford, having an unanticipated adulthood can present some unique challenges for cystic fibrosis patients. Whitford is a journalist based in Princeton, New Jersey. He writes for the *Guardian, Newsweek*, and *Slate*.

W hen 6-month-old Tiffany was diagnosed with cystic fibrosis in 1972, her doctor warned her mother not to let her play with dolls. The girl would die before her 5th birthday, he said; why stir up maternal instincts she could not hope to fulfill? But by the time Tiffany reached 5, new treatments had arrived, and the doctors promised her a few years longer. It was to be the first of many reprieves as medical advances kept barely a step ahead of the growing girl. At 10, doctors said Tiffany would die in adolescence; at 18, she abandoned her dream of going to college because she did not expect to live to graduate. "I can't remember a time when I didn't know I was supposed to die," says Tiffany, now 33, who lives in Bradenton, Fla., with her husband, John Reid, and their three children. "But I'm still proving them wrong."

## Life-Extending Treatments

When cystic fibrosis was first diagnosed in the 1930s, 80 percent of its victims died before their 1st birthday as their bodies' mucus thickened, clogging their lungs and digestive tracts. But . . . since the 1990s, new treatments have extended patients' life spans from months to years, and from years to decades. Cystic fibrosis is still the most lethal genetic disorder in America, affecting 30,000 people, but most sufferers now do not succumb until their mid-30s; a lucky few reach old age. With 40 percent of patients now older than 18, a new generation is living to face the challenges—both medical and emotional—of an adulthood nobody thought they would see.

The gift of life has come in installments. The extended life span of today's CF patients stems not from a single breakthrough but from a stream of minor innovations. Patients now stave off infection with a battery of different treatments: aerosols deliver increasingly potent antibiotics directly to their lungs; vibrating vests loosen their phlegm; fistfuls of enzyme supplements maintain their failing digestive tracts. "It's been an incredible success story, but we still have a lot of ground to cover," says Dr.

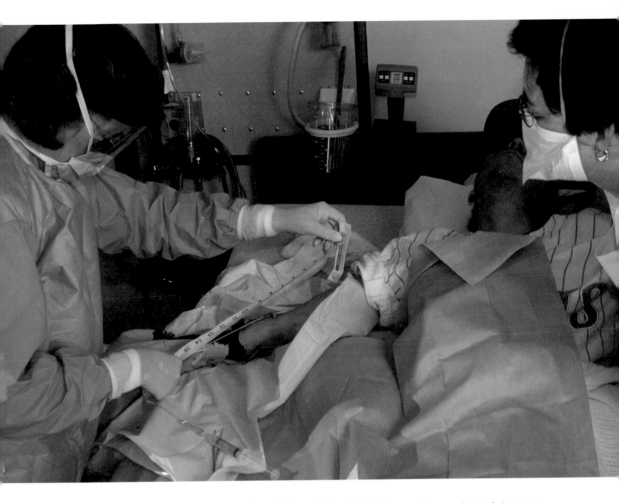

Bruce Marshall, [vice president] for clinical affairs at the Cystic Fibrosis Foundation. And despite new therapies targeting the deadly double-CF gene (carried in harmless single form by 10 million Americans), researchers say no decisive victory is imminent.

One of the new techniques used in treating CF is inserting a catheter for antibiotic therapy into the patient, which allows intravenous access for a prolonged period of time.

(© Phototake, Inc./Alamy)

## Futures They Never Thought They Would Have

Doctors have sometimes been slow to realize the implications of their success. Until recently, patients in their 30s were still treated in pediatric wards, sitting in the same Winnie the Pooh chairs they had used as children. Dozens

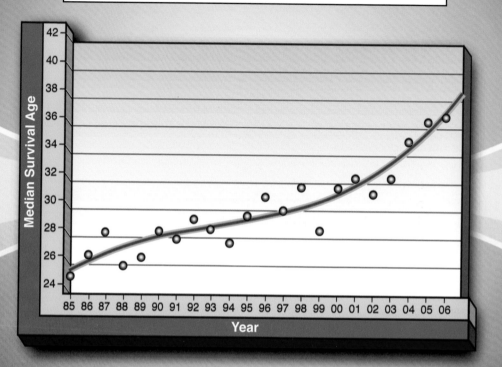

## Cystic Fibrosis Patients: Median Predicted Survival Age, 1985–2006

Median Survival Age

Year

Taken from: Cystic Fibrosis Foundation, *Patient Registry 2006 Annual Report*, Bethesda, MD.
© 2008 Cystic Fibrosis Foundation.

of adult centers have now opened, but the years in limbo left a mark, says Dr. Mike Knowles, codirector of the University of North Carolina's adult CF center. "Patients were sort of lost," he says. "They were not treated as if they were going to have a future, so they were not given the opportunity or responsibility to grow into mature young adults."

David Trester, a 32-year-old machine operator from Winona, Minn., blames cystic fibrosis for a youth spent drinking, fighting and racking up credit-card debt he never believed he would have to pay. "I was living in the fast lane," he says. "I didn't expect to live, so I figured, why not go out and enjoy every minute I can?" He reformed only when doctors told him potent new drugs meant he might live for decades—if his spiral into alcoholism and taste for Marlboros [cigarettes] didn't kill him first. "As I got into my late 20s I realized, hey, I'm going to live," says Trester, who is now alcohol-free, married and expecting his first child. "I figured it was time to clean up my act."

As they embrace adult life, more and more CF patients are starting families, but the path to parenthood can be tough. Though few male CF patients can father children without expensive surgery, many young men were never told they were infertile. Female patients, in contrast, can conceive relatively easily, despite the predictions of some doctors that the disease would leave them sterile. There was initial confusion, too, over whether patients' children would inherit CF; doctors now know that transmission is impossible unless both partners carry a defective gene, and screening has become widely available only . . . [since 2000].

Women with cystic fibrosis who decide to become pregnant believe they can survive long enough to raise their children. (AP Images)

## CF Is Still Fatal

And while genetic tests bring some peace of mind, prospective parents still face an agonizing dilemma. Despite medical advances, cystic fibrosis remains a fatal disease, and doctors often have to remind patients that they may not survive to raise their children. Pregnancy and sleepless nights strain patients' health, and exposure to schoolyard sniffles can trigger life-threatening infections in a parent's CF-ravaged lungs. "The easy part is getting pregnant," says Dr. Michael Boyle, director of the Johns Hopkins adult CF program. "Our job is to get patients to think more than nine months at a time."

For those who decide to have children, parenting can be both deeply fulfilling and bittersweet. Stacy Danko, a 40-year-old Baltimore mother of three, says she never regrets her decision; still, it's difficult watching her children, ages 14, 10 and 7, struggle to accept that their mother will die before her time. "I see their pain and it kills me," Danko says. "Your children are going to suffer as much as you do." And learning to live with that is the hardest thing of all.

# Gene Therapy and Genetic Research May Provide New Cystic Fibrosis Treatments

## National Human Genome Research Institute

In the following article the National Human Genome Research Institute (NHGRI) discusses how mutations in a single gene—the cystic fibrosis transmembrane regulator (CFTR) gene—result in a defective protein that affects cellular salt balance. According to the NHGRI, replacing defective CFTR genes with normal genes using gene therapy offers the best hope for a cystic fibrosis cure. Unlike most therapies, which treat the symptoms of disease, gene therapy eliminates the cause of disease. Cystic fibrosis patients who were successfully treated with gene therapy would have normal CFTR genes, normal CFTR proteins, and restored cellular salt balance. Despite its promises, gene therapy requires further research and development before it can be used to successfully treat CF or any other disease. The NHGRI is working to help researchers overcome these obstacles. The National Human Genome Research Institute, the federal government's lead genetic research agency, is devoted to research that attempts to understand the structure and function of the human genome and its role in health and disease.

SOURCE: "Learning About Cystic Fibrosis," National Human Genome Research Institute, National Institutes of Health, October 11, 2007.

Cystic fibrosis (CF) is the most common, fatal genetic disease in the United States. About 30,000 people in the United States have the disease. CF causes the body to produce thick, sticky mucus that clogs the lungs, leads to infection, and blocks the pancreas, which stops digestive enzymes from reaching the intestine where they are required in order to digest food.

## Cystic Fibrosis: A Single Gene Disease

Mutations in a single gene—the Cystic Fibrosis Transmembrane Regulator (CFTR) gene—cause CF. The gene was discovered in 1989. Since then, more than 900 mutations of this single gene have been identified.

In normal cells, the CFTR protein acts as a channel that allows cells to release chloride and other ions. But in people with CF, this protein is defective and the cells do not release the chloride. The result is an improper salt balance in the cells and thick, sticky mucus. Researchers are focusing on ways to cure CF by correcting the defective gene, or correcting the defective protein.

## FAST FACT

The following American groups carry at least one abnormal CFTR gene: 1 in 25 people of Northern European decent; 1 in 17,000 African Americans; and 1 in 30,000 Asian Americans.

## Gene Therapy Research Offers Promise of a Cure for Cystic Fibrosis

Gene therapy offers great promise for life-saving treatment for CF patients since it targets the cause of CF rather than just treating symptoms. Gene therapy for CF had its start in 1990, when scientists successfully corrected faulty CFTR genes by adding normal copies of the gene to laboratory cell cultures.

In 1993, the first experimental gene therapy treatment was given to a patient with CF. Researchers modified a common cold virus to act as a delivery vehicle—or "vector"—carrying the normal genes to the CFTR cells in the airways of the lung.

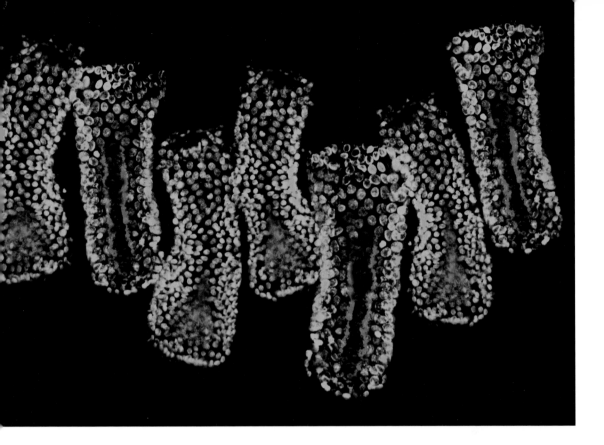

Subsequent studies have tested other methods of gene delivery, such as fat capsules, synthetic vectors, nose drops or drizzling cells down a flexible tube to CFTR cells lining the airways of lungs. Researchers are now testing aerosol delivery using nebulizers.

An immunofluorescence micrograph of intestinal glands shows the distribution of cystic fibrosis transmembrane regulator (CFTR) in red. (Phototake, Inc./Alamy)

But finding the best delivery system for transporting normal CFTR genes is only one problem that scientists must solve to develop an effective treatment for CF. Scientists must also determine the life span of affected lung cells, identify the "parent cells" that produce CFTR cells, find out how long treatment should last and how often it needs to be repeated.

The first cystic fibrosis gene therapy experiments have involved lung cells because these cells are readily accessible and because lung damage is the most common, life-threatening problem in CF patients. But scientists hope that the technologies being developed for lung cells will be adapted to treat other organs affected by CF.

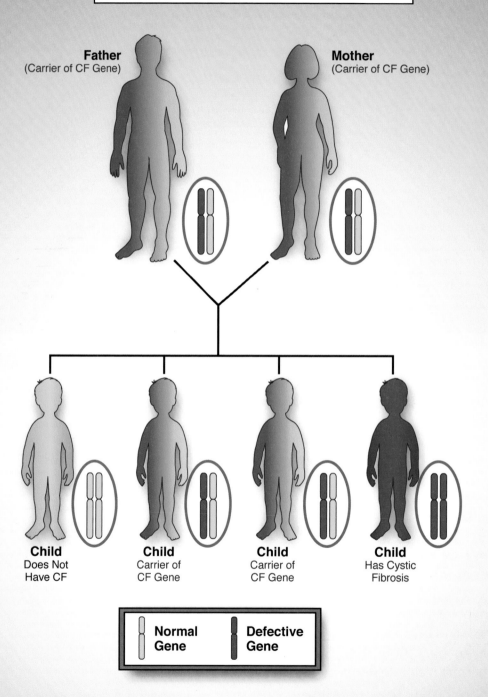

# Inheritance of Cystic Fibrosis

**Father**
(Carrier of CF Gene)

**Mother**
(Carrier of CF Gene)

**Child**
Does Not
Have CF

**Child**
Carrier of
CF Gene

**Child**
Carrier of
CF Gene

**Child**
Has Cystic
Fibrosis

**Normal Gene**

**Defective Gene**

Taken from: Neonatal Diseases eLibrary, Web-books.com, attributed to National Heart, Lung and Blood Institute.

Another research breakthrough offers a promising approach to treating cystic fibrosis. Researchers at the University of Washington's Genome Center and at Patho-Genesis Corporation have completed a genetic map for the *Pseudomonas aeruginosa* bacterium. This bacterium is the most common cause of chronic and fatal lung infections for people with CF. Scientists hope to use their knowledge of this bacterium's genetic sequence to develop innovative drugs for treating infections caused by *P. aeruginosa.*

As the amount of information about CF grows, scientists have recognized the need to share their research findings. To facilitate this sharing of information, the Cystic Fibrosis Foundation funds Cystic Fibrosis Foundation Therapeutics, Inc.–National BioInformatics Center (CFFTI-NBC) located at the University of North Carolina, Chapel Hill. The center is becoming a repository for data derived from gene expression studies. By pooling information, researchers hope to accelerate the process of finding a cure for CF.

## Testing for Cystic Fibrosis

CF has a variety of symptoms, including very salty-tasting skin, a persistent cough and excessive appetite but poor weight gain. The "sweat test"—which measures the amount of salt in sweat—is the standard diagnostic test for those with symptoms. A high salt level indicates CF.

But one in 31 Americans—more than 10 million people—are symptom-less carriers of the defective CF gene and can pass on the defective gene to their children. To develop CF, a child must inherit a defective gene from both parents. If both parents are carriers, there is a 25 percent chance that each child they conceive will have CF, and a 50 percent chance that the child will be a carrier.

The purpose of carrier testing—a laboratory test done on a sample of blood or saliva—is to see if a couple is at risk for giving birth to a child with CF. Carrier testing is not infallible. It cannot detect all of the CF gene mutations. In rare cases, a person can have a normal test result and still be a CF carrier.

If both parents are carriers, they may want to consult with a genetic counselor for help in deciding whether to conceive or whether to have a fetus tested for CF.

Prenatal testing for CF can be done around the 11th week of pregnancy using chorionic villus sampling (CVS). This involves removing a tiny piece of the placenta. Or, the fetus can be tested with amniocentesis, around the 16th week of pregnancy. In this procedure, a needle is used to take amniotic fluid surrounding the baby for testing. Since CF cannot be treated before birth, the purpose of prenatal testing is to prepare parents to care for a baby with special health needs, or to make a decision about terminating the pregnancy.

# A Common Food Preservative Might Help Cystic Fibrosis Sufferers

## Karen McNulty Walsh and Mona S. Rowe

In the following article Karen McNulty Walsh and Mona S. Rowe of the U.S. Department of Energy's Brookhaven National Laboratory (BNL) describe a potential new cystic fibrosis treatment that uses sodium nitrite, a common food preservative. According to the authors, researchers at BNL and at the University of Cincinnati found an unexpected weakness in cystic fibrosis patients' biggest foe—*Pseudomonas aeruginosa*. *P. aeruginosa* is one of the most common forms of bacteria found in the lungs of cystic fibrosis patients. Researchers found that *P. aeruginosa* is easily destroyed with sodium nitrite, a common food preservative. Walsh and Rowe are writers and media specialists for Brookhaven National Laboratory, one of ten national laboratories overseen by the U.S. Department of Energy.

**SOURCE:** "Common Food Preservative Might Provide Treatment for Cystic Fibrosis," Health News, University of Cincinnati Academic Health Center, Public Relations & Communications, news release, (http://healthnews.uc.edu), January 26, 2006. Reproduced by permission.

Researchers led by a University of Cincinnati (UC) scientist say they have discovered what might be the "Achilles' heel" of a dangerous organism that lives in the lungs of cystic fibrosis patients—a fatal flaw that leaves the organism vulnerable to destruction by a common food preservative.

It has been known for some time that the bacterium, *Pseudomonas aeruginosa*, grows within the deadly, lung-clogging mucus found in the airways of cystic fibrosis patients and significantly weakens them.

## Reason for Hope: Antibiotic-Resistant Killer Has Weakness

The new study suggests, however, that a mutation—known as mucA—in the organism also represents a fatal flaw that could help physicians clear the characteristic "goop" from the lungs of advanced cystic fibrosis patients.

The reason for optimism, the researchers say, is that the same genetic change that turns *Pseudomonas aeruginosa* into a sticky, antibiotic-resistant killer also leaves it susceptible to destruction by slightly acidified sodium nitrite, a common chemical that is widely used in the curing of lunch meat, sausages and bacon.

The finding is reported in the February 2006 edition of the *Journal of Clinical Investigation* by a 15-member U.S. and Canadian team headed by Daniel Hassett, PhD, an associate professor in UC's molecular genetics, biochemistry and microbiology department. The research was funded by the U.S. National Institutes of Health, the Cystic Fibrosis Foundation and the U.S. Department of Energy.

"We believe that we have discovered the Achilles' heel of the formidable mucoid form of *Pseudomonas aeruginosa*, which could lead to improved treatment for cystic

> **FAST FACT**
>
> Currently more than 25 clinical trials are ongoing for people with cystic fibrosis.

fibrosis airway disease," said Dr. Hassett. "We can essentially say that this organism, which some people thought could never be beaten, can now be destroyed by nothing more exotic than a common food preservative."

Cystic fibrosis, which affects about 30,000 people in the United States, mostly Caucasians of north European origin, is an inherited disease caused by a defect in a gene called the cystic fibrosis transmembrane conductance regulator (CFTR). Affecting the airways and many other vital organs and processes, cystic fibrosis is chronic, progressive and ultimately fatal, mostly as a result of respiratory failure.

"The lung-clogging, suffocating mucoid form of *Pseudomonas aeruginosa* essentially is a death sentence for cystic fibrosis patients because these bacteria are inherently antibiotic and white-cell resistant," said Dr. Hassett.

Until the 1980s, most deaths from cystic fibrosis occurred in children and teenagers. Today, thanks to improved treatments, people with cystic fibrosis live an average of 35 years.

## Tissue-Killing Biofilm

"During the chronic form of cystic fibrosis," Dr. Hassett said, "the mutated form of the organism, combined with the immune system's attempts to fight it off, wreaks havoc in the lungs. When *Pseudomonas aeruginosa* invades the mucus that's built up in the airways," said Dr. Hassett, "it forms a resistant 'biofilm,' like that which occurs on teeth or a toilet bowl, and divides rapidly.

"White cells from our immune system try to get in there to fight off the invaders," he added,

> but they can't reach the bacteria to kill them because they're enmeshed in that thick mucus, essentially a human form of "quicksand." So in trying to defend the body against . . . *Pseudomonas aeruginosa*, the white

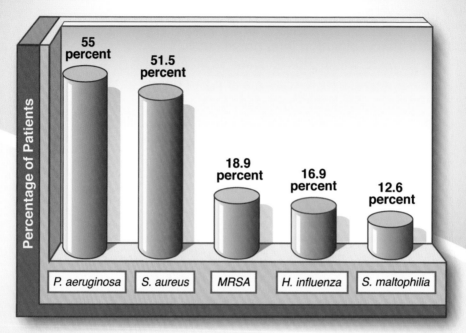

## Common Infectious Bacteria in Lungs of Cystic Fibrosis Patients, 2006

Percentage of Patients

- 55 percent — P. aeruginosa
- 51.5 percent — S. aureus
- 18.9 percent — MRSA
- 16.9 percent — H. influenza
- 12.6 percent — S. maltophilia

Taken from: Cystic Fibrosis Foundation, *Patient Registry 2006 Annual Report*, Bethesda, MD.
© 2008 Cystic Fibrosis Foundation.

blood cells end up dumping toxic, damaging material onto the airway surfaces, which leads to lung destruction. This biofilm lines the whole area, getting thicker and thicker and developing into a dense layer that deprives surface tissue of oxygen, ultimately killing it. So it's not only the bacteria that contribute to the disease, it's also our own immune system.

## Mucoid Bacteria Easily Destroyed

The good news is that Dr. Hassett and his colleagues found that about 87 percent of the mucoid *Pseudomonas* organisms they studied have a "fatal flaw" in the very gene (mucA) that makes it mucoid as well as antibiotic and immune-system resistant—they are easily destroyed by slightly acidified (pH 6.5) sodium nitrite.

Part of the problem with early and chronic cystic fibrosis, Dr. Hassett explained, is that patients with these conditions make very little nitric oxide, a derivative of acidified sodium nitrite.

"Mucoid *Pseudomonas aeruginosa* bacteria should have enzymes that are able to dispose of both nitrite and nitric oxide," Dr. Hassett said, "but for whatever reason, this particular bug doesn't make them, or has very low levels of them. That's the fatal flaw in mucoid *Pseudomonas aeruginosa*."

## A Surprising Finding

Dr. Hassett and his colleagues had worked on the hypothesis that the mucoid bacteria—because they flourish in patients who are essentially drowning in their own airway mucus—would grow better using nitrate or nitrite as an alternative to the missing oxygen. But when they tested nonmucoid and mucoid forms, the nonmucoids grew with both nitrate and nitrite without oxygen, while the mucoid organism grew only with nitrate, yet died with nitrite.

The team took about 60 mucoid bacteria from six different clinics in the United States and Canada and found that of all the strains that were mucoid, the ones that had mucA mutations were all sensitive to nitrite, and those that are notoriously antibiotic resistant were even more sensitive.

"Sodium nitrite kills the mucoids, and if nonmucoids or other bacteria are present in the airways, it inhibits their growth too," said Dr. Hassett. "When we add slightly acidified sodium nitrite to a suspension containing mucoid bacteria, it's converted to the gas nitric oxide," said Dr. Hassett. "The mucoid bacteria can't dispose of the nitrite metabolically, and also have difficulty handling the gas, so they die."

"Here was something we hypothesized that would allow mucoid bacteria to grow much better than nonmucoid

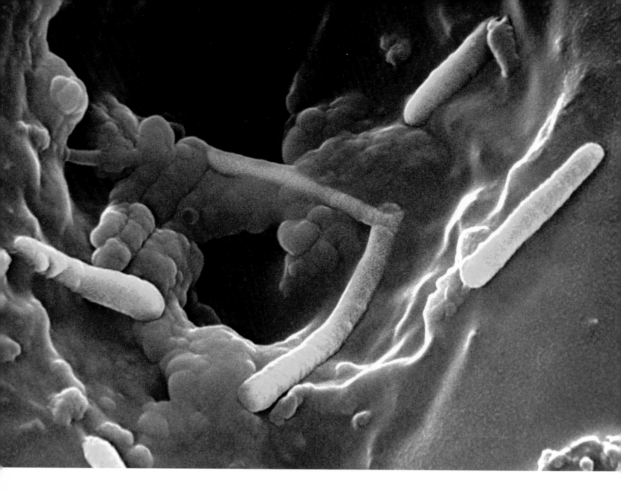

An electron micrograph shows the rod-shaped bacteria *Pseudomonas aeruginosa* in yellow. Researchers have found that sodium nitrite, a common food preservative, destroys the bacteria. (© Phototake, Inc./Alamy)

bacteria, but instead it killed them," said Dr. Hassett. "In plain English, these bacteria had a defect that we didn't anticipate. I've never been so happy in my life to be wrong!"

## Treatments Need Development

Sodium nitrite, Dr. Hassett said, has potential as "a time-release" capsule for cystic fibrosis patients. Because the nitrite is degraded very slowly, and mucoid bacteria can't get rid of it, it should specifically kill mucoid organisms that have the mucA mutation—which most do.

Dr. Hassett said he envisions sodium nitrite could be used in aerosol form to treat mucoid *Pseudomonas aeruginosa* in cystic fibrosis lung disease. "This wouldn't need to be a long-term treatment," he said. "Once a patient acquires mucoids, which commonly occur, the physician would simply use sodium nitrite and monitor how many mucoid bacteria are still in airway sputum. Once the mucoid organisms are killed, and the patient starts showing signs of improvement, treatment would continue with conventional antibiotics."

But bringing this treatment to the bedside won't be easy, Dr. Hassett conceded. "Right now, we don't see the Food and Drug Administration approving blowing sodium nitrite into people's airways, because it may potentially have some toxic side effects. However, nitrites are used clinically, to counteract cyanide poisoning, warts and athlete's foot, for example. And in neonatal pulmonary hypertension, physicians may be using nitrite doses nearly 60 times higher than we use to kill the organism in mouse and human airway cells."

# Many Cystic Fibrosis Patients Also Suffer from Diabetes

## Medical News Today

The following *Medical News Today* article discusses the results of a 2006 study suggesting that cystic fibrosis–related diabetes (CFRD) is different from other kinds of diabetes. Type 1 and type 2 diabetes, which combined affect more than 20 million Americans, are caused by the body's failure to produce insulin or to use it properly. The diabetes that afflicts people with cystic fibrosis shares characteristics of type 1 and type 2 diabetes. However, researchers at the University of Florida have found that it has a different cause. *Medical News Today* says more research is needed to help the 25 percent of adolescents and 40 percent of adults with CF who have CFRD. *Medical News Today* is one of the largest independent health and medical news Web sites on the Internet.

A growing number of cystic fibrosis patients are battling a second, often deadly complication: a unique form of diabetes that shares characteris-

SOURCE: "Cystic Fibrosis-Related Diabetes Studied by UF," *Medical News Today*, July 10, 2006. Copyright © 2006 MediLexicon International Ltd. Reproduced by permission.

tics of the type 1 and type 2 versions that strike many Americans.

Many of these patients are teens who take enzymes to help digest their food and undergo daily physical therapy to loosen the thick, sticky mucus that clogs their lungs. But despite treatments that are helping thousands to live decades longer than ever before, when diabetes strikes, their life expectancy plummets—on average by two years for men and an astounding 16 for women.

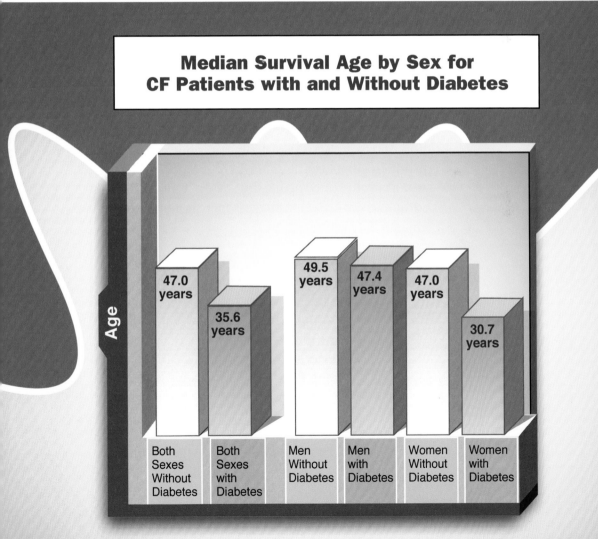

**Median Survival Age by Sex for CF Patients with and Without Diabetes**

Taken from: Carlos Milla, Joanne Billings, and Antoinette Moran, "Diabetes Is Associated with Dramatically Decreased Survival in Female but Not Male Subjects with Cystic Fibrosis," *Diabetes Care*, September 2005.

## Cystic Fibrosis-Related Diabetes Unique

Now a University of Florida (UF) study in animals suggests diabetes in cystic fibrosis patients is not caused by the destruction of insulin-producing cells in the pancreas—as is often the case in patients with the traditional form of type 1 diabetes—but by differences in how these cells function. The findings were published [in July 2006] in the American Diabetes Association's journal *Diabetes*.

Cystic fibrosis patients with diabetes produce some insulin on their own, but they require daily injections to boost their levels when eating so they can properly use sugar and other food nutrients for energy. At times they also become very resistant to the insulin they do make, similar to people with type 2 diabetes.

"For the longest time, the development of diabetes in cystic fibrosis has been thought to be chronic destruction of pancreas, so eventually you get loss of the insulin-producing beta cells," said Michael Stalvey, M.D., an assistant professor of pediatrics at UF. "Our study provides some early evidence to suggest there is an inherent difference in beta cell function."

## CF-Related Diabetes Is Becoming More Common

Cystic fibrosis patients suffer recurrent episodes of infection and inflammation that slowly destroy the lungs. The pancreas is also affected, interfering with proper digestion. The disease stems from a faulty gene that blocks the normal passage of salt and water through the body's cells. It is this gene deficiency that is proposed to cause insulin-producing cells to malfunction, Stalvey said.

About 30,000 Americans have cystic fibrosis, making it the nation's most common lethal hereditary disorder. On average,

## FAST FACT

The prevalence of CFRD in the United States jumped from 4.4 percent in 1992 to 12 percent in 2002, a 173 percent rise.

they will not live past 35, though some are living through their 40s and even into their 60s. As each year passes, the likelihood they will develop diabetes increases. As many as 16 percent of all patients with cystic fibrosis also have diabetes, a number that is expected to rise as overall life expectancy for cystic fibrosis patients increases. Half will show signs of diabetes by age 30 and will suffer a rapid decline in overall health and lung function, muscle mass and body mass index.

A scientist at Altus Pharmaceuticals works on developing a synthetic pancreatin for cystic fibrosis patients to help insulin-producing beta cells in the pancreas. (© Rick Friedman/ Corbis)

"It's becoming more and more frequent because of the increasing age of patients," Stalvey said. "That's part of the reason why new recommendations call for screening patients 14 years and older yearly with an oral glucose tolerance test. Each year we know their likelihood of developing diabetes gets higher and higher.

"These young people, teenagers or young adults in their early 20s, have been fighting all their lives to stay healthy and keep their nutrition up," he added. "Now they've just been given something that potentially will overwhelm them. It's a huge thing for them, given the consequences that diabetes means to their underlying condition."

## Studying Cystic Fibrosis–Related Diabetes Is Important

In the UF study, researchers developed the first animal model for the study of cystic fibrosis-related diabetes. They used mice that scientists from the University of North Carolina engineered to be missing the gene that makes the protein responsible for transporting salt and water across the cell membrane. People with cystic fibrosis have a mutated form of this protein.

UF scientists administered a low dose of a chemotherapy drug that weakened insulin-producing cells but did not destroy them. They then tested the animals' ability to regulate their blood sugar while fasting and after receiving glucose, simulating the rise in blood sugar that occurs after eating food.

Animals with the protein deficiency were more sensitive to the effects of the chemotherapy drug and had more difficulty regulating blood sugar levels, both while fasting and after receiving glucose. Mice that were still able to produce the crucial protein that prevents cystic fibrosis were able to maintain normal blood sugar levels, even after the drug had damaged some of their insulin-producing cells.

"This goes beyond improving our understanding of patients with cystic fibrosis-related diabetes; it also will help us improve our understanding of other forms of diabetes and help us work on strategies for a future cure," Stalvey said.

"Twenty-five percent of adolescents and 40 percent of adults with cystic fibrosis have diabetes, and diabetes is associated with poorer survival in this population," said Antoinette Moran, M.D., division head of pediatric endocrinology and director of the Pediatric Diabetes Program at the University of Minnesota Medical School. "The cause of cystic fibrosis-related diabetes is not completely understood, but it is clearly different from other forms of diabetes. The study by Stalvey and colleagues is important because it is the first to show that there are intrinsic abnormalities in the insulin-producing cells of the pancreas related to the genetic defect that causes cystic fibrosis."

# Lung Transplants May Be the Last Option for Some Cystic Fibrosis Patients

**Jane E. Brody**

In the following article Jane E. Brody asserts that progressive medical research has provided many life-extending treatments to cystic fibrosis patients. However, until a cure is found, lung failure eventually occurs for those suffering from the disease. Brody says that in order to survive cystic fibrosis, people must be as healthy as possible and must dedicate themselves to fighting the host of bacteria that are constantly trying to infect their lungs. However, lung failure is inevitable even for the healthiest and treatment-conscientious cystic fibrosis patients. Brody is health and medical writer for the *New York Times*.

More than 10 million people in this country carry in all their cells one copy of a defective gene that regulates the movement of sodium, chloride and water in and out of cells.

These people are, on the surface, perfectly healthy. But when two such carriers of this defective gene have children, they have a 25 percent chance that each child will inherit an abnormal gene from each parent and will be born with cystic fibrosis.

The result of a defective protein, cystic fibrosis is a chronic, progressive and ultimately fatal disease that clogs the lungs and pancreas with thick, sticky mucus.

## Common Genetic Disease

About 30,000 people in the United States have cystic fibrosis, the most common life-shortening genetic disease among Caucasians worldwide. It occurs in 1 in 3,300 live births among whites, with a lower incidence in other groups. The incidence is highest, 1 in 2,500 births, among descendants of Northern European whites and Ashkenazi Jews.

How has such a lethal gene survived the throes of evolution? Just as carriers of the sickle cell gene have a survival advantage because their abnormal gene offers some protection against malaria, some scientists believe that carriers of the cystic fibrosis gene were better able to survive the often fatal diarrhea caused by cholera.

> **FAST FACT**
>
> Research suggests that people with CF who live in households with lower incomes are more likely to have poorer lung function.

At least 800 different defects, or mutations, are known to occur in this critical gene, which causes a cell to create a protein called the cystic fibrosis transmembrane conductance regulator, or C.F.T.R. Different mutations cause different disruptions of the regulator's role, and, as a result, different degrees of severity of cystic fibrosis.

The most common mutations disrupt the movement of C.F.T.R. from its point of origin to its site of operation and cause a severe and ultimately fatal disease.

## Research Makes a Difference

As recently as 25 years ago, most children born with cystic fibrosis died in early childhood and few survived to their teenage years. Today, most can expect to live past 30. Many finish high school and college, get jobs and have families.

The difference stems from productive research, the results of persistent fund-raising efforts and pressure from parents, who established the Cystic Fibrosis Foundation in 1955. The research led to an understanding of the way cystic fibrosis causes life-threatening damage through a chain of events that involves damaged genes, abnormal tissues and malfunctioning organs.

This understanding, in turn, has led to the development of preventive techniques and treatments that can attack every stage of the disease process. New treatments now in development promise even further gains.

Some experts predict that within a decade, the lung damage from cystic fibrosis will be limited by periodic gene therapy in children and young adults. Better yet, some say, will be the application of techniques already technically feasible to correct the defect genetically even before a child is born, or soon enough afterward to prevent tissue damage. Only then might researchers begin to talk cautiously of cure.

## Survival Dependent on Host of Therapies

Meanwhile, a host of therapies to forestall complications have become the focus of survival for patients with cystic fibrosis.

Respiratory physical therapy done two or more times a day to loosen the thickened mucus, enabling it to be coughed up, is essential to maintaining the ability of the lungs to transfer oxygen and carbon dioxide. In years past, clapping on the chest, back and sides was the only method. Now the job can be done by inhaled nebulizers, vibration vests and a flutter device that is blown into, freeing a patient from daily dependence on a lay or professional therapist.

Because the thickened mucus is a breeding ground for bacteria, antibiotics are another critical factor in maintaining pulmonary health. With mucus coating the small airways in the lungs, the hair cells are unable to clear out invading bacteria.

The trick has been staying ahead of the ability of microorganisms to develop resistance by continually finding new antibiotics to which they are still susceptible. The potentially deadly infections mean frequent hospitalizations for many cystic fibrosis patients. Some have a central line implanted to aid in the frequent administration of antibiotics.

Malnutrition is a constant risk because ducts clogged by mucus are unable to move digestive enzymes to sites where food is broken down and absorbed. Thus, enzyme-packed pills to aid digestion and fat-soluble vitamin supplements

A young mother uses a nebulizer to help loosen the mucus in her daughter's lungs, allowing her to breathe without distress. (Joey McLeister/MCT/ Landov)

(A, D, E and K) are other daily requirements for maintaining the health of people with the disease.

Another problem is consuming enough calories to compensate for the effort expended in breathing with congested lungs.

Dehydration is yet another risk because the defective gene causes an abnormal absorption of sodium, dehydrating the lungs and making them more susceptible to infection. So people with cystic fibrosis have to be even more devoted to water bottles than aerobics instructors.

Experts on cystic fibrosis emphasize two other important factors in coping with the illness: building and maintaining physical stamina and obtaining psychological support for patients and their families. The stronger people are, physically and emotionally, the better able they are to handle the complications and treatments for the disease.

## Lung Failure Is Inevitable

But eventually, despite the best therapy available, the lungs of people with cystic fibrosis become too damaged to sustain life. When that critical time appears on the horizon, a growing number of patients seek a double-lung transplant, an operation as risky as a heart transplant. Both lungs are needed to prevent the transplanted one from becoming diseased.

When kidneys fail, dialysis can substitute for kidney function, but nothing similar exists for the lungs. There is no telling when lung failure will occur, necessitating a transplant. For some, like Stefanie Allen, it happened at age 11. For Charlie Tolchin, it was 28. For Michael Maggio, it was 40.

About 3,700 patients are on a lung transplant waiting list nationwide. But each year only about 1,000 receive transplants. The problem stems from an acute shortage of viable organs and a limited number of medical centers with staff members skilled at the procedure.

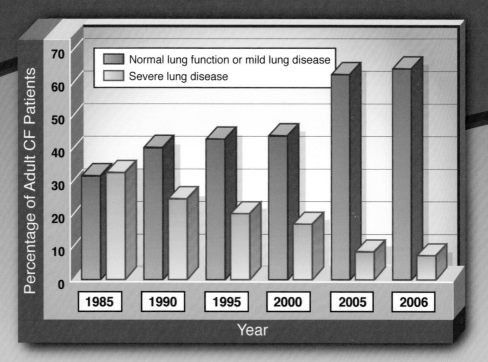

## Percentage of Adult Cystic Fibrosis Patients with Severe Lung Disease Is Decreasing

Taken from: Cystic Fibrosis Foundation, *Patient Registry 2006 Annual Report*, Bethesda, MD.
© 2008 Cystic Fibrosis Foundation.

The lungs have to be big enough to sustain the recipients. For some patients who are small, it is possible to use part of the lungs from two live donors, usually relatives.

The operation is expensive and risky: 5 percent of patients do not survive it. Three years after a transplant, 62 percent of the patients are still alive. The main problem is chronic rejection, which can occur despite the constant use of complication-prone immune-suppressive drugs. One complication is the development of lymphoma, a cancer of the lymph system that can be fatal, as it was for Mr. Maggio at 49.

# CHAPTER 2

# Controversies About Cystic Fibrosis

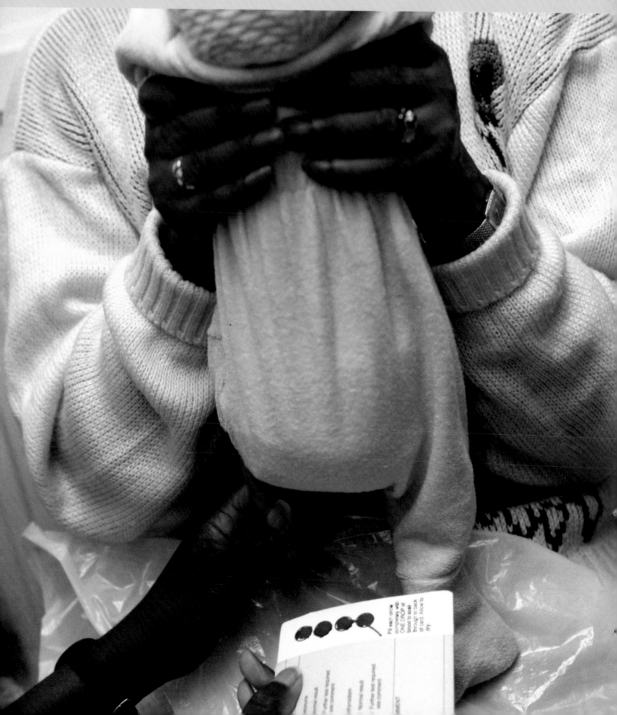

# Newborn Screening for Cystic Fibrosis Is Important

### Cystic Fibrosis Foundation

*In the following article the Cystic Fibrosis Foundation (CFF) urges all states to screen newborns for cystic fibrosis. Newborn screening began in the 1960s with testing for phenylketonuria (PKU). Today, every newborn in the United States is tested for PKU and a host of other genetic and metabolic diseases, such as hypothyroidism, galactosemia, sickle cell anemia in African American infants, and many others. It is generally up to each state to decide what newborn screening tests are performed. CFF says that screening for cystic fibrosis is justified and beneficial and gives children with cystic fibrosis the best hope for living healthy lives. CFF is one of the leading nonprofit cystic fibrosis organizations in the United States.*

The Cystic Fibrosis Foundation recommends that all states routinely screen for cystic fibrosis (CF) in all newborns. The Centers for Disease Control and

**SOURCE:** Cystic Fibrosis Foundation, "Newborn Screening Overview," Cystic Fibrosis Foundation, July 2, 2008. www.cff.org. Reproduced by permission.

*Photo on facing page. A newborn is given a Guthrie test at birth to detect phenylketonuria, an inborn error of amino acid metabolism related to cystic fibrosis. (© Sally and Richard Greenhill/Alamy)*

Prevention (CDC) published a similar recommendation in October 2004. The following . . . provide[s] more details about newborn screening for CF and explains why it is important for all states to include it in their programs.

More than 10 million Americans are symptomless carriers of the defective gene that causes CF and most are not aware of a family history of the disease. Research studies conducted over the past two decades have shown that early intervention with nutritional therapies provides distinct benefits including improved height, weight and cognitive function for people with CF. These therapies also may impact respiratory function and life expectancy, and reduce hospitalizations.

Specialized care and new CF therapies have improved the length and quality of life for people with this disease today and provide great promise for the lives of people with CF to come. With these possibilities for early treatment and healthier lives, it is imperative that states add CF to their newborn screening programs to give these children the best chance for a healthy future. . . .

## Newborn Screening Provides Best Chance for Healthy Future

Cystic fibrosis is a genetic disease that causes thick, sticky mucus to build up in the lungs and digestive system and other organs of the body. This mucus leads to chronic lung infections and difficulty digesting food and nutrients. The treatment of CF depends upon the severity of symptoms and the organs involved.

Most people with CF must take pancreatic enzyme supplements with every meal to absorb enough calories and nutrients to grow and stay healthy. They also must eat a high-calorie, high-fat diet. People with CF also perform daily airway clearance therapy to help clear mucus from the lungs. Other

**FAST FACT**

Approximately one in thirty-five hundred Caucasian children in the United States is born with cystic fibrosis each year.

types of treatments include antibiotics to fight lung infections and drugs to thin the mucus and improve lung function.

In recent years, many advances in the care and treatment of CF have improved the length and quality of life for people with the disease. The median age of survival for a person with CF is now nearly 37 years. For babies born with CF today, the chances of improved health quality and longevity are even greater.

By screening for CF in newborns, treatments can start before symptoms occur, which can enhance nutrition and minimize or delay complications, thereby giving newborns the best chance for a healthier future. . . .

## Benefits of Newborn Screening for CF

Newborn screening for CF is justified based on more than 20 years of strong, scientific evidence and observational

An infant is administered a "heel stick" PKU test at birth. The test is used to screen for many genetic and metabolic diseases. (© Picture Partners/ Alamy)

studies in the United States and abroad. This research has shown the importance of early diagnosis. Under current standards, most people with CF are not diagnosed until they show symptoms of the disease.

Early diagnosis allows for immediate intervention with specialized therapies, including pancreatic enzymes to aid digestion and a high-calorie, high-fat diet. These interventions have been shown to result in improved height, weight and cognitive function, and also may help maintain respiratory function, while increasing life expectancy and reducing hospitalizations. . . .

CF is caused by a recessive gene, which means that a child must inherit two copies of the defective CF gene—one from each parent—to have the disease. Even then, there is only a one in four chance that the child of two carriers will have CF. More than 10 million Americans are unknowing, symptomless carriers of the defective CF gene and most are not aware of a person with CF in their family history. . . .

A newborn screening test is not a diagnostic test. In fact, only a fraction of babies with an initial positive CF newborn screening test ultimately are diagnosed with the disease. If an initial screen is positive, further tests are done to rule out or confirm a CF diagnosis. . . .

For a disease to be included in newborn screening test panels, it should meet certain requirements and conditions. Some of the considerations are: benefits of early diagnosis; existence of accurate tests to confirm the diagnosis; and improved health because of early detection and timely treatments. CF meets all of these criteria.

The benefits of newborn screening for CF have been documented and studied extensively. New treatments and specialized care for CF have improved and extended the lives of people with the disease. In addition, research has shown that early diagnosis and proper care of babies with CF can have significant impact on their nutritional status throughout childhood and perhaps even into their late teens. This allows children with CF to grow and possibly develop to their genetic potential. . . .

## All States Should Screen Newborns for Cystic Fibrosis

The recommendations from the CF Foundation and the CDC urge all states to do newborn screening for CF and to establish a comprehensive program to ensure appropriate diagnostic and follow-up care for all those screened.

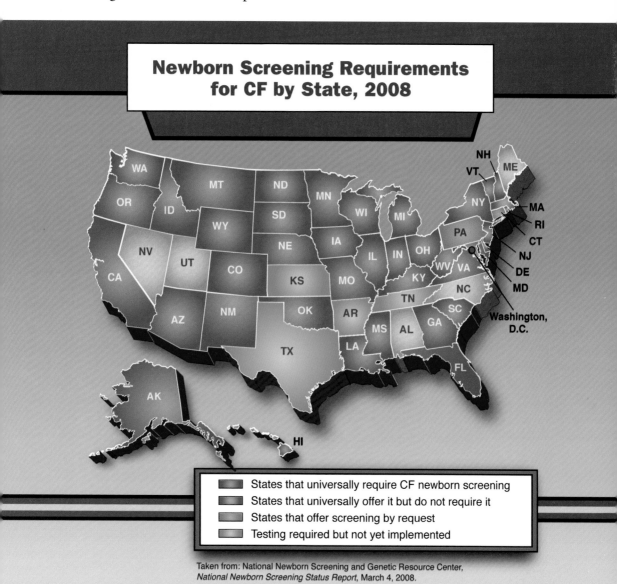

### Newborn Screening Requirements for CF by State, 2008

- States that universally require CF newborn screening
- States that universally offer it but do not require it
- States that offer screening by request
- Testing required but not yet implemented

Taken from: National Newborn Screening and Genetic Resource Center, *National Newborn Screening Status Report*, March 4, 2008.

There are several ways to encourage state governments to implement CF newborn screening programs. First, contact the state health department to find out if CF is being considered for newborn screening. Then, call or write the state governor to encourage support for the addition of CF screening. . . .

Screening for CF in all newborns is . . . important even if the carrier screening tests for parents were negative. CF carrier screening only identifies the most common of the more than 1,000 mutations of the defective CF gene. Although it is unlikely for a child to have CF in this situation, it is still a possibility. Therefore, it is still important that all newborns be given the newborn screening test for CF. . . .

Babies born with CF today will benefit from already approved therapies that have extended survival for people with CF to nearly 37 years. They also will benefit from other therapies to come, which—we are confident—will help them live quality lives into their 40s, 50s and beyond.

The CF Foundation has more than 25 potential therapies in various stages of pre-clinical development and clinical trials. Any of these potential treatments, if successful, could make a profound difference in the lives of people with CF.

The CF Foundation will continue to work on these potential therapies while also adding new therapies to the development pipeline. We are dedicated to adding tomorrows every day for all people with CF.

# Newborn Screening Has Downsides

## CBS News

*In the following article from CBS News, the authors report on a downside to newborn screening. The authors say that false-positive results for newborn screening tests are rising and unnecessarily alarming new parents. A study showed that the parents of babies who received false-positive results worried more about their child and about their own parenting skills months after finding out the tests were wrong. Additionally, the study found that false-positive results impacted the relationship parents felt they had with their child. The authors say that providing parents with more information about the newborn screening process would help alleviate some of the stress associated with false-positive newborn screening results. CBS News is one of the largest news networks in the United States.*

Virtually all babies in the U.S. have their heels pricked soon after birth to get a blood sample for genetic testing. These "heel stick" tests identify

SOURCE: CBS News, "Genetic Tests Stress Out New Parents," CBSnews.com, June 5, 2006. Copyright © 2006 by MMVI The Associated Press. All rights reserved. Reproduced by permission.

rare metabolic disorders before they can cause irreversible damage. But as more disorders are added to the screening—many states now test for 30 or more—false-positive results are on the rise.

In the June [2006] issue of *Pediatrics*, researchers from Children's Hospital Boston report that false-positive results cause considerable parental stress, even when the baby proves negative on retesting, and that the stress could be alleviated by better education for parents and pediatricians.

Psychologist Susan Waisbren, Ph.D. and Elizabeth Gurian, M.S. in Children's Division of Genetics interviewed 173 families who had received false-positive screening results and a comparison group of 67 families with normal newborn screening results.

## Lingering Effects of Incorrect Results

Although mothers in the false-positive group were interviewed at least six months after their child's diagnosis had been ruled out, they reported more worry about their child's future and rated themselves less healthy than mothers in the comparison group.

Fifteen percent said their child needed extra parental care, versus 3 percent of mothers in the comparison group. After adjustment for socioeconomic factors, both mothers and fathers in the false-positive group had higher scores on the standardized Parenting Stress Index (PSI); 11 percent of mothers (versus no mothers in the comparison group) scored in the clinical range, in which treatment might be prescribed.

Waisbren and Gurian also found that false-positive tests affected the parent-child relationship: parents in the false-positive group scored more highly on two subscales of the PSI: a Parent-Child Dysfunctional

## FAST FACT

In 2005, Iowa and New York tested newborns for forty-six different disorders, while Arkansas, Kansas, Montana, Utah, and West Virginia required only four newborn screening tests.

## Estimated Number of False-Positive Test Results for Selected States, 2005

Data are based on newborn screening tests being 99.995 percent accurate.

| State | False Positives |
|---|---|
| California | 626 |
| Colorado | 79 |
| Georgia | 35 |
| Illinois | 181 |
| Maryland | 63 |
| Michigan | 32 |
| Missouri | 62 |
| Nevada | 35 |
| New Jersey | 57 |
| New York | 288 |
| Ohio | 119 |
| Texas | 19 |
| Wisconsin | 70 |
| Wyoming | 0 |

Taken from: Beth Tarini, Dimitri Christakis, and Gilbert Welch, "State Newborn Screening in the Tandem Mass Spectrometry Era: More Tests, More False-Positive Results," *Pediatrics*, August 1, 2006.

Interaction scale and a Difficult Child scale. (The first asks parents to rate their agreement with statements like "I expected to have closer and warmer feelings for my child, and this bothers me"; the second has statements such as "My child makes more demands on me than most children.")

Waisbren believes a positive test result can increase expectations of illness even when it is later found to be in error. "We're not sure why—maybe it feeds into a general nervousness as new parents," she speculates. "But our results also show that parental stress was greater when families didn't have adequate information and understanding."

## Lack of Information Increases Stress

Two-thirds of parents with false-positive results did not correctly understand why their child was called back for a repeat test, the study found. Mothers who knew the correct reason had reduced stress. (This was not true for fathers, however.)

Other findings:

- Some parents had to wait as long as a month to get the result of the second test, and 26 percent voiced concerns about the length of time before a diagnosis was ruled out.
- Half of all parents in the false-positive group said they hadn't been told, or didn't remember being told, that the diagnosis had been ruled out.
- Of these, 22 percent said they were told they wouldn't be notified unless a problem was found, and 24 percent were required to ask their pediatrician for the test results. "A few parents didn't even know they'd had a repeat test," Waisbren says.
- Sixty-one percent of parents felt a need for more information about newborn screening and the test result.

The researchers suggest that improved and better-timed education may reduce parental stress related to newborn screening. "There needs to be a specific communication plan for informing parents at every step," Gurian says. "Currently, pediatricians are the primary distributors of this information, but some pediatricians don't feel knowledgeable enough about these rare metabolic disorders to explain a positive test to a parent. It would be good to begin involving obstetricians and to begin educating parents about newborn screening during the prenatal period."

The study was funded by the Maternal and Child Health Bureau of the U.S. Health Resources and Services Administration and the Ethical, Legal and Social Implications (ELSI) division of the Human Genome Project, National Institutes of Health.

Experts say the amount of stress parents endure because of newborn screening can be reduced by a specific communication plan that informs parents at every step.
(© **thislife pictures/ Alamy**)

According to the CDC [U.S. Centers for Disease Control and Prevention], more than 4 million babies born in the U.S. each year undergo screening for biochemical genetic disorders, with severe disorders detected in about 3,000. One recent study suggests that there are at least 12 false-positive results for every true case diagnosed; another puts the ratio at more than 50-to-1.

# Genetic Testing for Cystic Fibrosis Should Be Routinely Offered

## R. John Massie, Martin B. Delatycki, and Agnes Bankier

In the following viewpoint R. John Massie, Martin B. Delatycki, and Agnes Bankier contend that the Australian government should establish a national cystic fibrosis (CF) carrier screening program and encourage pregnant couples and those planning a pregnancy to take the test. CF carrier testing identifies people who carry a defective cystic fibrosis gene. Millions of people carry one copy of a mutated cystic fibrosis gene. If two carriers marry and have children, the chances are one in four that their baby will have cystic fibrosis. The authors contend that Australia has implemented widespread carrier testing for many other diseases and there is no reason CF should not be added to the list. They believe Australia should follow the lead of the U.S. government and recommend that all pregnant couples be offered carrier testing for cystic fibrosis. Massie, Delatycki, and Bankier are fellows of the Royal Australasian College of Physicians.

SOURCE: R. John Massie, Martin B. Delatycki, and Agnes Bankier, "Screening Couples for Cystic Fibrosis Carrier Status: Why Are We Waiting?" *Medical Journal of Australia*, vol. 183, 2005, pp. 501–502. Copyright © 2005 Medical Journal of Australia. Reproduced by permission.

T he technology for safe, cheap screening for the principal gene mutations responsible for cystic fibrosis has long been available. Nearly 10 years ago [1997], the US National Institutes of Health recommended "testing for gene mutations that cause [cystic fibrosis] be offered as an option to all pregnant couples and those planning a pregnancy." A similar recommendation has been made by a joint committee of the American College of Obstetricians and Gynaecologists and the American College of Medical Genetics. In 1998, [the *Medical Journal of Australia*] published an editorial emphasising the need for Australia to follow suit in promoting carrier screening for cystic fibrosis. There has been little response despite the fact that each year 70 babies are born in Australia with cystic fibrosis, almost all to parents with no family history.

## FAST FACT

The American Board of Genetic Counseling has certified about sixteen hundred genetic counselors since 1993.

## Better to Offer CF Screening Before Couples Have First Baby

Cystic fibrosis is the most common severe autosomal recessive disease of childhood, with an incidence of 1 in 2500 and carrier frequency of 1 in 25. Clinical manifestations include progressive, irreversible suppurative lung disease and pancreatic exocrine insufficiency. Although most children with cystic fibrosis can expect to survive into adulthood, the daily therapies are rigorous, and there are many years of ill health. The median life expectancy is in the mid-30s, with end-stage lung disease the major cause of death. There is still no cure.

Most patients with cystic fibrosis are detected by newborn screening, using a biochemical test (for immunoreactive trypsinogen [IRT]) for all babies, followed by cystic fibrosis gene mutation analysis for those with a raised IRT level. Newborn screening facilitates the early diagnosis of cystic fibrosis and genetic counselling for affected families. Couples identified with an affected infant can choose prenatal testing using gene mutation analysis from a chorionic villus sample for subsequent pregnancies to ascertain the status of the fetus.

The genetic test used for diagnosis of cystic fibrosis and prenatal testing can also be used to identify carriers of a cystic fibrosis gene mutation. Testing for cystic fibrosis gene mutations is reliable, and, with a 12-mutation panel, nearly 85% of possible severe mutations can be

A technician prepares cultures of amniotic cells taken from pregnant women. They will be analyzed for cystic fibrosis and other genetic disorders. (©AGStockUSA, Inc./ Alamy)

detected. It can be performed using a painless cheek swab. However, testing for carrier status is generally not offered in Australia to couples without a family history, and most of those who carry a mutation do not know until an affected child is born. While we acknowledge the benefits of newborn screening, we believe it would be better to offer cystic fibrosis gene mutation screening to all couples, before they had their first baby with cystic fibrosis.

## Prenatal Screening Is Common

Prenatal screening for a variety of conditions is routine in Australia. All women have a full blood count early in pregnancy, and those who are iron replete with a low mean cell volume are tested for thalassaemia carrier status. The outcome is that it is now uncommon for babies to be born with thalassaemia. Prenatal screening for Down syndrome (using a combination of ultrasound examination and measurement of serum markers) has been offered since 1996, and more than two-thirds of pregnant women in Victoria participate in this screening. Populations with a high frequency of genetic conditions such as Tay–Sachs disease are also offered prenatal or preconceptual screening. Paradoxically, the carrier frequency of cystic fibrosis in the general Australian population is almost the same as the carrier frequency of Tay–Sachs disease in the Ashkenazi Jewish population. Lack of awareness about cystic fibrosis no doubt contributes to the lack of community pressure to screen.

A successful prenatal screening program for cystic fibrosis has been pursued in Edinburgh for many years. This program uses a model of couple testing for carrier status with the offer of prenatal genetic testing of the fetus when both partners are carriers and has halved the incidence of cystic fibrosis in that community. Uptake of the service is 80%, similar to the uptake in a smaller Dutch study. In Victoria, 67% of couples with an infant with cystic fibrosis have used prenatal testing for subsequent pregnancies. Some families have opted for pre-implantation genetic diagnosis (with in-vitro fertilisation technology) to avoid pregnancy termination.

## CF Screening Should Be Offered Universally in Australia

We advocate a cystic fibrosis screening program in which both parents are encouraged to be screened at the same time, which will give the most accurate risk assessment of the couple having a baby with cystic fibrosis. Ideally, screening would be performed before conception, to allow the couple time to decide on the best reproductive option. In reality, many women do not present for pre-pregnancy

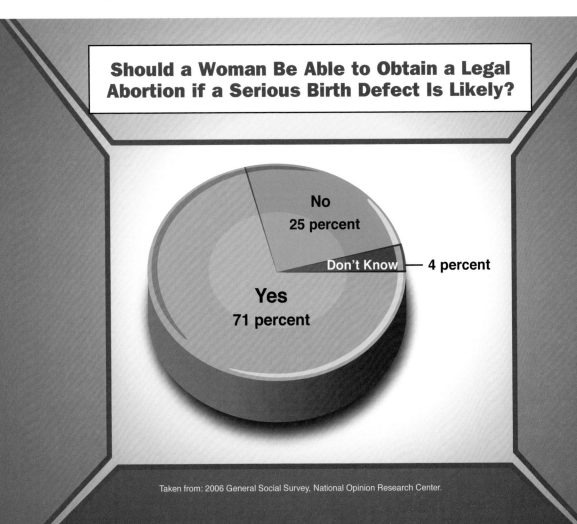

**Should a Woman Be Able to Obtain a Legal Abortion if a Serious Birth Defect Is Likely?**

No
25 percent

Don't Know — 4 percent

Yes
71 percent

Taken from: 2006 General Social Survey, National Opinion Research Center.

assessment, so a screening model that allows prenatal testing of the couple should remain available. Furthermore, we advocate that both parents receive their individual carrier result to maximise the opportunities for cascade family testing. Any program offering carrier screening needs to include genetic counselling for carrier couples, individual carriers and relatives of carriers who may also wish to be tested.

Extensive data clearly demonstrate the cost effectiveness of cystic fibrosis screening. The lifetime cost of care for a patient with the condition outweighs the cost of screening women of child-bearing age.

Cystic fibrosis carrier screening should be a federal initiative [in Australia]. Currently, the care of patients with cystic fibrosis and the newborn screening programs are state funded, and there is little incentive for a national program. A Medicare-rebatable test would allow universal access and encourage uptake. Surely, it is time to fund carrier screening for cystic fibrosis in Australia.

# Genetic Testing Is Worrisome and Should Not Be Routinely Offered

### Richard W. Sams

In the following viewpoint Richard W. Sams contends that widespread use of carrier and prenatal testing for cystic fibrosis is problematic. He says that women are often pressured to terminate pregnancies based on testing results that are complex and often interpreted incorrectly. As a result, many healthy babies are aborted. The notion that babies are aborted for even the possibility of having a genetic disease worries Sams. He believes that carrier and prenatal testing are indicative of a society that is moving toward a new kind of eugenics, where children are viewed merely as commodities. Richard W. Sams is a family physician in the U.S. Navy and the director of the navy's Family Medicine Residency Program in Jacksonville, Florida.

Cystic fibrosis (CF) is a hereditary disease that affects much of the body, especially the lungs and digestive system, leading eventually to disability

**SOURCE:** Richard W. Sams, "Faces Disappearing: The Implications of Cystic Fibrosis Screening," *New Atlantis*, Summer 2007, pp. 129–33. Copyright © 2007 Ethics and Public Policy Center. All rights reserved. Reproduced by permission. See www.TheNewAtlantis.com for more information.

and death. The disease runs its course very differently in different patients; some have severe pulmonary and gastrointestinal problems starting in the first year of life, while others have relatively mild symptoms until adolescence. Lung disease is usually the primary factor in determining the quality and length of a patient's life; about 90 percent of all people with CF die from pulmonary complications. Since cystic fibrosis generally doesn't impair cognitive functioning or musculoskeletal development, it is possible for patients with mild cases to lead relatively normal lives; a 1995 survey reported that 35 percent of young adults diagnosed with CF work full-time and 90 percent had completed high school. Thanks to therapeutic advances in recent decades, the median survival age of patients has been steadily rising: According to the Cystic Fibrosis Foundation, in 1976 it was 18 years, in 1995 it was 30.1 years, and in 2005 it was 36.8 years.

## Newborn Screening Morphs into Prenatal Testing

About 30,000 Americans have cystic fibrosis, and around 1,000 new cases are diagnosed each year. The disease is most common among Caucasians, with an incidence of 1 in 3,500 live births (compared to roughly 1 in 12,000 in non-white populations). Our understanding of the genetic causes of the disease have improved; since 1989, over 1,300 mutations of a particular gene have been linked to CF. These discoveries have made it possible to use genetic tests to determine if expecting parents are unwary carriers of a cystic fibrosis mutation, or to determine if a person actually has the disease—so parents with afflicted newborns, for instance, can know about the disease before symptoms are manifest. A workshop convened by the Centers for Disease Control in 1997 recommended such neonatal CF screening, calling it a "paradigm for public health genetics policy development."

Two years later, in 1999, a panel put together by the National Institutes of Health (NIH) recommended that CF screening be pushed further back from neonatal care to prenatal care. The NIH panel published a statement intended to give health care providers, patients, and the general public a "responsible assessment of the optimal practices for genetic testing for cystic fibrosis" so that individuals would be able to obtain enough information to make "informed decisions." The panel recommended that health care providers offer cystic fibrosis testing to adults with a family history of CF, to partners of people with CF, to couples planning a pregnancy, and to couples seeking prenatal care. In 2001, following the lead of the NIH, the American College of Obstetricians and Gynecologists (ACOG) issued an essentially identical set of recommendations, in the form of guidelines and educational materials distributed to ACOG members.

## Prenatal CF Testing Now Common

Since the publication of the ACOG guidelines, cystic fibrosis testing has become an increasingly common part of prenatal care. About a year after the guidelines were published, *OB/GYN News* reported that leading commercial genetic and diagnostic testing laboratories performed between 300,000 and 500,000 CF carrier tests in the United States. While that figure represented a tripling, quadrupling, or in one case an elevenfold increase, in testing volumes at those labs when compared with 2001, it was still far short of ACOG's "target levels," since the number of tests was "dwarfed by the approximately 4 million live births a year in the United States."

For expecting parents, a carrier test is either a one-step (both the woman and the man are tested simultaneously) or a two-step process (the woman is tested first; if she is a carrier, the man is then tested). If both are carriers, an amniocentesis or chorionic villus sampling is performed to test the unborn child. There are no definite statistics

Doctors perform amniocentesis on a pregnant woman. The prodecure can reveal the presence of a number of genetic defects. (Phototake Inc./Alamy)

on the number of cystic fibrosis tests now performed on fetuses in the United States, but it is clear that prenatal CF testing is quickly joining the so-called "quadruple screen," a common regimen of tests that look for chromosomal abnormalities (Down syndrome in particular) and neural tube defects. If a prenatal test shows that a fetus has inherited both parents' mutations, the unborn

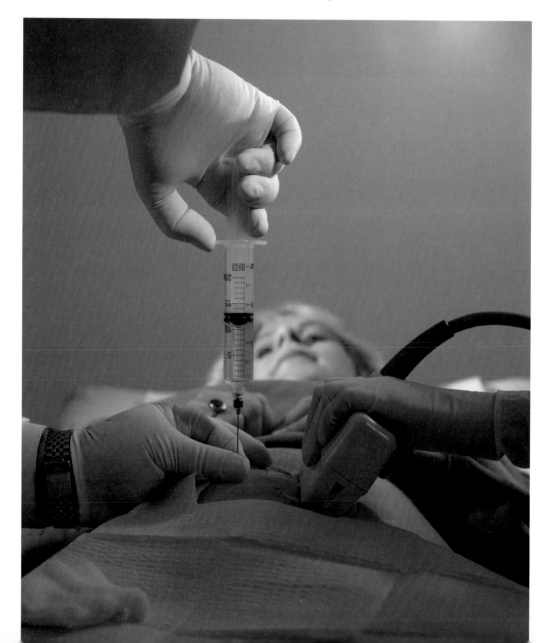

child is classified as having cystic fibrosis. The parents are then usually referred to genetic counseling, either from a licensed genetic counselor or, more frequently, from their OB-GYN, to receive information about the disorder, the prognosis, and the available treatment options.

## Predicting CF Prognosis Difficult, Parents Typically Uninformed

In practice, however, such counseling is woefully inadequate. The test results are especially tricky to interpret: a child may have a CF genotype, but it is unclear how the disease would be phenotypically expressed. The NIH statement on this issue points out that identifying the specific CF mutation is not "highly predictive of the severity and course of pulmonary disease, which is the major factor affecting patient quality of life and longevity." Some men with "a high frequency of CF mutations" are healthy but for sterility caused by a genital deformation; some women with CF mutations "are normal or develop chronic sinusitis or bronchitis as the extent of their morbidity," according to the NIH. "It is unclear whether such mildly affected individuals can be reliably identified by their genotype." In other words, an unborn child who tests positive for CF may have minimal if any symptoms or may ultimately have extensive life-shortening pulmonary disease. It is possible to predict the extent of pancreatic insufficiency, but not possible to predict the extent of the symptoms that would have the greatest effect on the child's life.

This inability to predict the extent of the disease is highly significant for genetic counselors trying to communicate with parents. In a 2002 review of the state of prenatal CF testing for the *Journal of Pediatrics*, Philip M. Farrell and Norman Fost conclude:

Many couples will undoubtedly benefit, but there is reason for concern about the potential for harm, and uncertainty about how many couples will be making truly informed choices. CF is one of the most complex single-gene disorders with extraordinary genotypic and phenotypic variation coupled to an evolving, inexorably improving array of therapies. Communicating information about prognosis is a daunting challenge, especially for health care professionals with limited experience in managing patients with CF, as is the case with most obstetricians.

Farrell and Fost note that geneticists believe it would require a trained counselor an hour or more to convey the necessary information. It is unlikely that this is happening in busy obstetrical practices. Given the complexities of the diagnosis in the prenatal period, the meaning of the diagnosis once it is made, and the likelihood that insufficient information is being conveyed, there is great potential for doing more harm than good. Such genetic counseling is inadequate at best, and may be irresponsible.

## Abortion Assumed to Be an Appropriate and Cost-Effective Option

More fundamentally, while the NIH and ACOG do not claim any moral standpoint on abortion, they recommend widespread testing in the interest of "helping people make informed decisions." They assume abortion is an appropriate response to physical or mental disability, and this perspective is built into genetic counseling. That has certainly proven true in the case of Down syndrome. Currently, roughly 90 percent of the fetuses that test positive for Down syndrome in the United States are aborted. "For me, it's just faces disappearing," the mother of a daughter with Down syndrome recently told the *New York Times*. The rapid mainstreaming of prenatal CF testing is poised to follow precisely the same course.

Even though early diagnosis can be immensely beneficial in providing a couple with information to begin treatment before the child develops symptoms, newborn screening would suffice for this. The prenatal test is explicitly designed to diagnose CF in order to give the patient the option to abort the child—and by simply offering it, the clinician is, at some level, morally sanctioning abortion.

While the NIH and ACOG policy recommendations are formally neutral on the subject of abortion, some of the reasoning supporting those recommendations explicitly connects cystic fibrosis testing to the supposed economic benefits of ending pregnancies—employing the language of cost-benefit analysis to rationalize aborting fetuses diagnosed with CF. The NIH report matter-of-factly notes the amount of money that our already-strained health care system will save by aborting fetuses with cystic fibrosis: "studies showed that the cost per identified CF fetus averted ranged from $250,000 to $1,250,000 for a Caucasian population of Northern European ancestry"; the "direct and ancillary costs associated with a CF birth" are estimated at $800,000.

> **FAST FACT**
>
> In a 2006 study reported in the journal *Pediatrics*, 56 percent of women surveyed reported that they would be likely to terminate a pregnancy if prenatal testing revealed cystic fibrosis.

## Women Often Feel Pressured

Although the NIH and ACOG statements stipulate that CF screening should be strictly voluntary, women often feel pressured to have prenatal genetic testing done. Frequently, doctors simply order the tests as part of the "routine standard of care." And if previous experience with other prenatal tests is any guide, as CF testing becomes more common, it will lead inevitably to more abortions. As a physician, I have personally had patients tell me they were pressured by other physicians to have prenatal tests—or even to abort their babies. One woman for whom I provided prenatal care had a child diagnosed with a severe heart anomaly by ultrasound at 20 weeks gestation. The anomaly is virtually always lethal. Both a perinatologist and a geneticist recommended to the couple that the woman have an abortion. Despite being deeply offended by the recommendation and informing the physicians that she would carry the child to term, the suggestion was repeated numerous times. Her experience is far from anomalous. One woman's account in a survey published in 1999 by the Royal Association for Disability and Rehabilitation is a case in point:

> I was pregnant last year and came under severe pressure from every medical professional I saw about my decision to have no tests. Even when I pointed out that they were talking to a disabled person about the possibility of eliminating her child if it was disabled, they could not see how offensive it was.

## Healthy Babies Aborted

As . . . prenatal screening techniques grows, such intolerance will only deepen—a problem made even more vexing by the grim fact that some of the fetuses being aborted today were wrongly diagnosed. At a meeting of the President's Council on Bioethics in June 2006, Dr. Benjamin Carson, a pediatric neurosurgeon, cautioned that blanket testing isolated from clear purpose and moral understanding is gravely irresponsible:

> The question has come up [of] what have we historically done with data that we've acquired on newborns or prenatal individuals? . . . Almost all women in this nation now receive ultrasounds during the course of their pregnancy and you know, a number of things can be picked up on those ultrasounds, one of which is hydrocephalus. And almost uniformly, when there is an indication of hydrocephalus a recommendation for termination is made. . . . A significant number of those patients who decide not to go the abortion route it turns out end up with children who are normal, who never required a shunt,

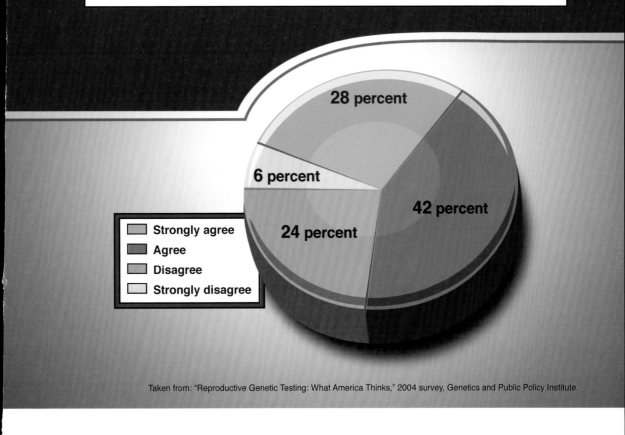

## The Ability to Control Human Reproduction Will Lead to Treating Children like Products

28 percent

6 percent

42 percent

24 percent

Strongly agree
Agree
Disagree
Strongly disagree

Taken from: "Reproductive Genetic Testing: What America Thinks," 2004 survey, Genetics and Public Policy Institute.

never required anything and yet had come to see me for a recommendation for abortion.

## We Are Moving Toward a New Eugenics

What is particularly chilling in Dr. Carson's remarks is that the assumption that disabled children must not be born is apparently so powerful that many babies who would have been completely healthy are being aborted as well.

In 1999, embryologist and IVF pioneer Robert Edwards said, "Soon it will be a sin for parents to have a child that carries the heavy burden of genetic disease. We are entering a world where we have to consider the quality of our children." Such considerations are becoming ever more routine. Discussing nascent life in the cold language of quality control and cost analysis, pressuring mothers to inspect their unborn children for potential defects, ending pregnancies because of the mere possibility that the child might be imperfect—this is the direction we are headed, toward a new eugenics. We must resolutely decide to take another course.

# Lung Transplants Extend Life for Many Cystic Fibrosis Patients

## American Thoracic Society

In the following article from the American Thoracic Society, the authors conclude that cystic fibrosis patients who undergo lung transplants are better off than those who do not get new lungs. The majority of deaths attributed to cystic fibrosis are the result of severe lung disease. The article cites researchers who conducted a study that looked at cystic fibrosis patients who were on a lung transplant waiting list in St. Louis, Missouri. The researchers found that those patients who received lung transplants lived on average 4.5 years longer than those who were still waiting. The American Thoracic Society is an organization of health professionals who specialize in lung-related areas of medicine.

Lung transplantation increases the survival of patients with cystic fibrosis by almost 4.5 years on average, according to a study presented at the

SOURCE: American Thoracic Society, "Study Finds Lung Transplants Increase Survival of Cystic Fibrosis Patients by More than Four Years," ScienceDaily.com, May 25, 2004. Reproduced by permission.

American Thoracic Society International Conference in Orlando on May 24 [2004].

"Initially the risks from lung transplantation for cystic fibrosis patients are quite high, but the risk drops over time, and it becomes worth the risk in the long run," said study co-author Roger D. Yusen, MD, MPH, Assistant Professor of Medicine in the Divisions of Pulmonary and Critical Care Medicine and General Medical Sciences at Washington University School of Medicine in St. Louis.

## CF Patients with Severe Disease Must Have a Double Lung Transplant

Cystic fibrosis (CF) is the most common lethal genetic disease in Caucasians, but it affects all races and ethnic groups. The disease affects about 30,000 people in the United States. Approximately 1,000 new cases are diagnosed every year. People with CF live an average of 33

Theresa Kloet has had two lung transplants to combat her cystic fibrosis and is living testimony to advances in cystic fibrosis treatments. (Merissa Ferguson/Newhouse News Service/Landov)

years. They develop severe lung disease, with a combination of airway obstruction, infection, and inflammation that accounts for the majority of deaths from the disease.

CF patients who receive lung transplants to treat their disease must have a double lung transplant in order for the surgery to be effective, said Dr. Yusen. Lung transplants are not common—approximately 1,000 are performed each year in the United States, and only 150 of them, or 15%, are performed on CF patients. "In the United States, lungs are distributed to patients on the waiting list based primarily on their waiting time, whereas the system for patients waiting for heart or liver transplant depends highly on medical urgency," explained Dr. Yusen.

However, a proposal currently being considered prioritizes patients on the waiting list for lung transplantation based on the medical urgency and the probability of survival after transplantation.

> **FAST FACT**
>
> In 2006 there were 362 deaths from cystic fibrosis out of 24,487 patients in the Cystic Fibrosis Foundation Patient Registry.

## CF Patients with Lung Transplants Live Longer

Dr. Yusen and colleagues studied all patients with CF who were on the waiting list for lung transplantation at Washington University School of Medicine and Barnes-Jewish Hospital in St. Louis since the program began in 1988. The study included 247 patients, who were followed through 2002. Most were Caucasian, reflecting the CF population as a whole, and the average age at the time of placement on the waiting list was 28. All the patients had severely impaired lung function and severe symptoms when they were placed on the waiting list.

Of the 247 patients in the study, after one year, 84% of patients were alive while waiting for a transplant, and an equal percentage were alive after having a transplant.

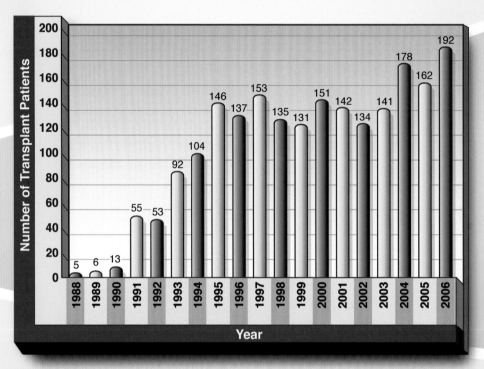

## Number of People with CF Who Received Lung Transplants, 1998–2006

Number of Transplant Patients (y-axis): 0, 20, 40, 60, 80, 100, 120, 140, 160, 180, 200

Year (x-axis):
- 1988: 5
- 1989: 6
- 1990: 13
- 1991: 55
- 1992: 53
- 1993: 92
- 1994: 104
- 1995: 146
- 1996: 137
- 1997: 153
- 1998: 135
- 1999: 131
- 2000: 151
- 2001: 142
- 2002: 134
- 2003: 141
- 2004: 178
- 2005: 162
- 2006: 192

Taken from: Cystic Fibrosis Foundation, *Patient Registry 2006 Annual Report*, Bethesda, MD.
© 2008 Cystic Fibrosis Foundation.

After two years, 67% of those waiting for a transplant were alive, compared with 76% who had a transplant. After five years, 55% of transplant patients were alive.

Though transplantation had a significant early death risk compared with continued waiting, the risks significantly decreased over time. Within 15 months, the survival benefit from transplantation became apparent. Based on an average survival of 5.7 years after transplant, the researchers determined that lung transplantation improved the life expectancy of patients with CF by almost 4.5 years.

"Next, we hope to see if transplanted patients are not only living longer, but enjoying a better quality of life than those who remain on the waiting list," Dr. Yusen said.

# Lung Transplants May Not Extend Life for Some Cystic Fibrosis Patients

**Ed Edelson**

In the following article Ed Edelson discusses a study suggesting that lung transplants may not be the best option for children. The study looked at children with cystic fibrosis who were on a lung transplant waiting list from 1998 to 2002. The findings of the study indicate that a very small number of children who receive lung transplants actually benefit from the procedure. The study authors tell Edelson that the study is controversial because many people do not like the results. They also tell Edelson that the guidelines used to determine who gets donated lungs when they become available have recently changed. Their study results and the new guidelines make what was already a very complex decision even more complicated, they say. Ed Edelson is a *Healthday* reporter. He was science editor for the *New York Daily News* for twenty years and has written more than twenty books on health and medical issues.

Hardly any of the children who receive lung transplants because of severe damage caused by cystic fibrosis benefit from the risky operation, a study concludes.

## Questioning Lung Transplant Benefits Is Controversial

It is a controversial conclusion, made more controversial because the transplant rules have been changed since the study was done, said Dr. Theodore G. Liou, associate professor of internal medicine at the University of Utah, and lead author of a report in the Nov. 22 [2007] *New England Journal of Medicine.*

CF is a hereditary disease in which the lungs and digestive tract become clogged with mucus. People with CF die at a relatively young age. Previous studies have shown some survival benefit for adult cystic fibrosis sufferers who received lung transplants as a last resort, Liou said.

The new report is one of very few looking at such transplants in children, he said. "In 2005, we published one [study] showing no difference in outcome between patients who were transplanted and those who were not, although they were equally sick as far as we could tell," Liou said. "That got us into a lot of trouble, because people didn't like the results."

The new study looked at 514 children with cystic fibrosis who were on the waiting list for lung transplants from 1992 to 2002. A total of 248 of the children did undergo the procedure during the study period.

## Small Number Received Benefits

The researchers found a significant estimated benefit for only five of those who had transplants, with "a signifi-

> **FAST FACT**
>
> From 1996 to 2005, death rates for both lung transplant candidates and recipients dropped, as did the time spent waiting for a lung transplant, according to the U.S. Organ Procurement and Transplantation Network and the Scientific Registry of Transplant Recipients.

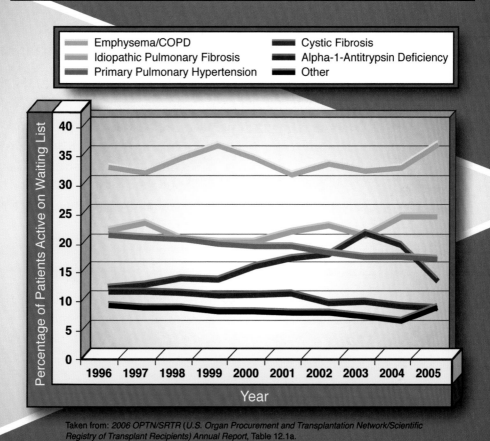

## Primary Diagnoses of Patients Active on the Lung Transplant Waiting List, 1996–2005

Legend:
- Emphysema/COPD
- Idiopathic Pulmonary Fibrosis
- Primary Pulmonary Hypertension
- Cystic Fibrosis
- Alpha-1-Antitrypsin Deficiency
- Other

Y-axis: Percentage of Patients Active on Waiting List
X-axis: Year (1996–2005)

Taken from: *2006 OPTN/SRTR (U.S. Organ Procurement and Transplantation Network/Scientific Registry of Transplant Recipients) Annual Report*, Table 12.1a.

cant risk of harm" associated with lung transplantation for 315 of the young patients, meaning that other treatment would have benefited them more.

The process has changed since the study was conducted, partly in ways that work against transplantation, Liou noted. Children selected for lung transplants now are first put on an intensive course of treatment intended to strengthen them for the surgery, he said, and "conventional treatments have gotten to be very good," he added.

The rules for actual performance of a transplant have also changed, said Dr. Julian L. Allen, chief of the division of pulmonary medicine at the cystic fibrosis center at the Children's Hospital of Philadelphia. He is also co-author of an accompanying editorial in the journal.

Until 2005, all children awaiting a lung transplant were placed on a single list, receiving organs as they became available. Now, the decision to transplant includes consideration of the patient's condition, with sicker children getting the operation sooner, Allen said.

"In some cases, children who were put on intensive therapy were deferred, because they got better," he said. "There was something about the children in that group who didn't get transplanted that made them get better."

Experts say a recent study on lung transplants to treat cystic fibrosis indicate that there is little difference in survival rates between patients who had transplants and those who did not. (**Peter Steffen/dpa/Landov**)

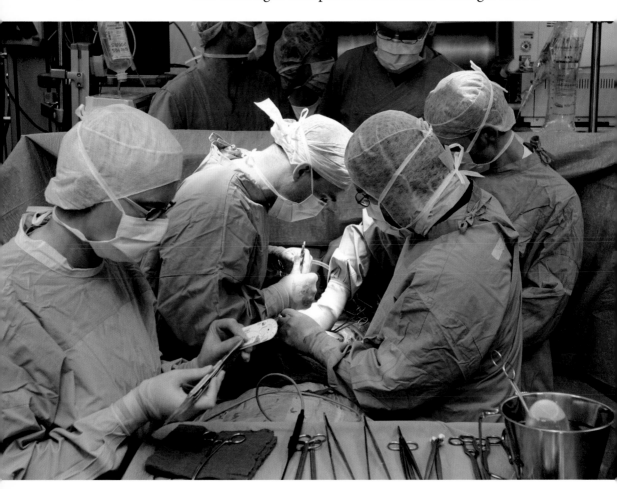

## Tough Decision Has Gotten Tougher

The bottom line, Liou said, is that a decision that has always been complex has gotten even more so. "Maybe people will pay attention and try to be more careful about selecting patients for lung transplants," he said. "You need to be careful about who you refer," Allen said. "You need to see if the results in this study hold true under the current rules. Also, the quality of life after a transplant has to be looked at. We need future studies that evaluate the quality of life."

One complicating factor with younger recipients of lung transplants is the need to be sure that they adhere to the strict regimen needed to prevent rejection of the organ, Allen added. The better success rate with older cystic fibrosis recipients is due partly to their better ability to follow instructions, he said.

# CHAPTER 3

# Personal Stories

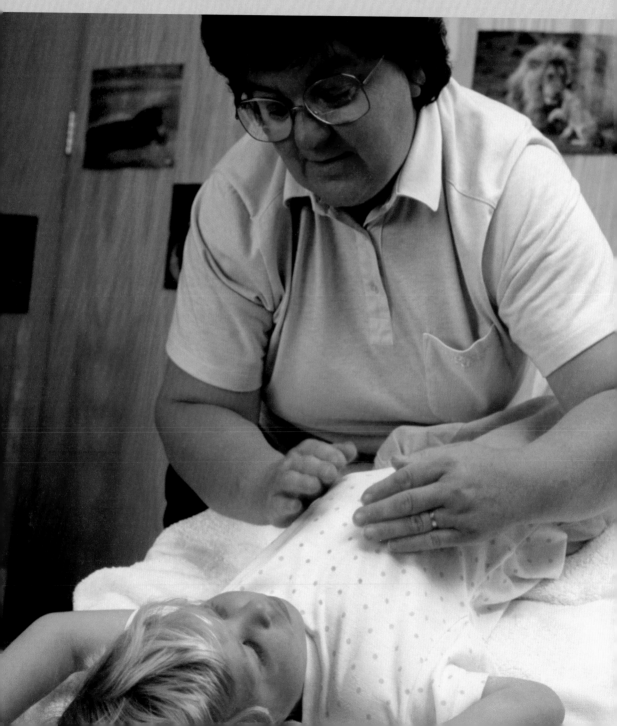

# Every Breath He Takes

### Roland Merullo

In the following article Roland Merullo tells the story of cystic fibrosis patient, living donor lung recipient, and surfer Matthew Joyce. Matt's cystic fibrosis did not become prominent in his life until high school. Then it almost killed him. He could not surf or run or do any of the things that teenage boys enjoy. Matt's lungs became infected with *Burkholderia cepacia*, an insidious and rare bacterium, which affects only a small percentage of cystic fibrosis sufferers. Because of *B. cepacia*, Matt was unable to obtain lungs from a deceased donor, which is the most common type of lung transplant. Merullo tells the amazing story of how two strangers stepped forward to donate parts of their own lungs to Matt. Living donor lung transplants are very uncommon. Matt still has cystic fibrosis but his new lungs have given him the gift of time. Because of the generosity of Matt's donors he is back to surfing and celebrating life. Roland Merullo is an author and the father of a child with cystic fibrosis. He has written several novels, one—*A Little Love Story*—about a young woman with cystic fibrosis.

*Photo on facing page.* A three-year-old cystic fibrosis patient receives percussion treatment from a physiotherapist. Percussion on the chest and back loosens the mucus, allowing it to be more easily expelled from the lungs. (Hattie Young/Photo Researchers, Inc.)

**SOURCE:** Roland Merullo, "Every Breath He Takes," *Reader's Digest*, December 2003. Copyright © 2003 by The Reader's Digest Association, Inc. Reprinted with permission from the Reader's Digest.

Floating just off the sandy crescent of California coastline at La Jolla Shores Beach, Matthew Joyce straddles a surfboard, facing out to sea. He studies the rhythm of the water—a gentle rise and fall, so similar to the rhythm of breathing—spots a wave he likes, turns the board and paddles hard. In two seconds he is standing, legs strong but thin as saplings, his curly brown hair lit up like a halo in the early morning sunlight. As the wave lifts him, he steps toward the board's nose, hangs ten, and then turns and dances in the other direction, a spider in a wet suit performing the difficult move surfers call a "walkback." He turns forward again and, as the wave dies in a burst of froth, expertly flips his board and drops into the water.

The whole performance takes less than a minute and looks like something Neptune's choreographer developed to demonstrate the joy of being alive. For 20-year-old Matt, surfing is a celebration of life. Three years ago [2000] he lay in a Los Angeles hospital "about as close to death as anybody I've seen who didn't die," says his doctor, Mark Pian. He was breathing with the help of a machine that pushed air into his diseased lungs. His weight had dropped to 70 pounds, and he was coughing up blood.

Unlike the three dozen other surfers in the water on this perfect morning, Matt has cystic fibrosis, a fatal genetic disease that afflicts about 30,000 Americans. But through a combination of medical technology, devoted doctors, the support of family and friends, Matt's own determination, and the remarkable sacrifice of two strangers, the young surfer is much more than just alive. On this fine day, Matt Joyce is breathing easy—through someone else's lungs.

A few hours after his morning surf, Matt sits in the backyard of his grandparents, Anthony and Frances Montisano. He pricks a finger to test his blood sugar level, and says, "All I wanted is what every other kid wanted, to be normal."

But normalcy is the first thing taken from people with cystic fibrosis. The disease has a simple cause: a defective gene that interferes with the normal movement of salt and water in and out of cells. The consequence of this—thick, sticky mucus—seems relatively benign until one considers the essential role mucus plays in the functioning of the lungs, pancreas and other organs. Just how essential may be evident very early. Many CF sufferers are diagnosed as infants because the thick mucous lining keeps pancreatic enzymes from getting to the intestines. Nutrients can't be properly absorbed and, in medical terminology, the infant "fails to thrive." This problem can be addressed with a regular intake of enzymes and vitamins, but, in later years, some people with CF develop painful bowel obstructions or, like Matt, diabetes.

Mucus plays an even more critical role in the lungs. Certain species of bacteria—harmless to healthy people—thrive in CF patients, forming infectious colonies that damage the lung tissue to the point where even a cold can be life-threatening. Eventually, the patient either gets a set of new lungs or suffocates.

There are at least 1,000 known mutations of the gene that causes CF, and every patient's symptoms are somewhat different. While there have been steady advances in treatment, some patients still die in their teens; others live into middle age, hold jobs, have children—even run marathons.

## Spiraling Downward

Matt was luckier than most, for a while. "I always knew I had CF, but I hid it," he says. Until eighth grade he was the fastest miler in his school. His father, Kevin, got him interested in bicycle motocross racing, and between the ages of 6 and 14, Matt and his brother, Joseph, were addicted to it. He played basketball, was on the cross-country team, learned to surf.

Then, in the summer after ninth grade, he was hospitalized for what he calls "a tune-up"—three weeks of IV antibiotics to control a lung infestation of a common bacterium in people with CF. In the tenth grade he was infected with a rare and more insidious bacterium called *Burkholderia cepacia* (only three percent of CF patients ever get it). He'd given up running, and now, stick-thin and weak, had to give up surfing.

By his senior year, Matt was on oxygen. He stopped going to classes, barely left his room. It was clear that the disease had progressed to the point where the only option was a lung transplant. But, looking at the poor survival data for patients with *B. cepacia*, physicians at his local hospital were unwilling to offer Matt the expensive transplant procedure. The circle was closing around him.

What happened next was a series of coincidences that Matthew's mother, Debbie, describes as a miracle. First, she took part in a CF walkathon and happened to meet a young woman who'd had a successful double-lung transplant, in spite of being infected with *B. cepacia*. Debbie and Kevin—who divorced when Matt was five years old but still remain friendly—sought a second opinion and met with Dr. Pian of the University of California, San Diego School of Medicine. Pian was more optimistic: He knew that surgeons at Childrens Hospital Los Angeles, two hours away, had done transplants on CF patients with *B. cepacia*.

In the midst of this hopeful news, Matt continued to spiral downward. On October 15, 2000, he was taken by ambulance to Childrens Hospital L.A., but it was obvious he wouldn't live to see his name at the top of the long list of people awaiting a new set of lungs. His only hope was a living-donor transplant, a procedure performed less than 30 times a year in America. The human lung is made up of two or three lobes; a living donor can give up one and still have nearly normal breathing capacity. To turn the hope of a transplant into reality, however, Matt's family had to find two compatible donors, each willing to endure the risks of major surgery.

Back to the string of coincidences. Frederick Phillips, a 55-year-old lawyer from San Diego, happened to be a regular customer at the La Jolla supermarket where Debbie worked. Debbie told Fred that Matt was sinking, and Fred, whose own stepson has CF but was doing well, volunteered to donate a lobe. Another donor—a woman who remains anonymous—also materialized, and for a brief moment it seemed Matt would have his second chance at life. But when she failed the last of a long list of pre-surgery tests, Matt's family began to prepare for his death.

Fortunately, a backup donor was being tested at that very hour. His blood type was compatible, he met the height and fitness criteria, and his pulmonary function tests were off the charts. This man, Dave Manglos, had come forward by a route some would call coincidental, others an act of providence.

> ## FAST FACT
>
> In 2005 only one of 1,405 lung transplant recipients received lungs from a living donor, according to the U.S. Organ Procurement and Transplantation Network and the *Scientific Registry of Transplant Recipients 2006 Annual Report.*

## Reborn

Manglos, then 40, was a special agent with the U.S. Customs Service. Driving back to San Diego a few days earlier after a morning assignment in L.A., he started feeling drowsy and pulled off the highway near the beach at San Onofre. There, he noticed a cluster of surfers in the water. He walked a ways, picked up some stones and started skipping them. Because the stone-skipping reminded him of being at church camp as a boy, he began to pray. And then: "I had this strong feeling that I was supposed to do something. I didn't know what it meant." He told no one—not his wife, children, or co-workers— about his moment on the beach. "I'm a cop," he says.

"I deal in concrete things. I thought people who had experiences like that were a little off the deep end."

The next night, he and his wife, Rhonda, watched the TV news, something they seldom do. Matt's cousin Jenny LaRocco came on to make an appeal for donors. Dave says, "Almost audibly I got this huge voice—you couldn't ignore it—saying, 'Didn't we talk about this yesterday?'" Jenny said they needed someone five-ten or taller, nonsmoker, O-positive blood. Dave looked at Rhonda. "That's me," he said.

Five days later, Dr. Vaughn Starnes, who pioneered the living donor lobar transplant in 1990, made a looping "clamshell" incision across Matthew Joyce's chest, sawed his patient's sternum in half, lifted the top of his chest wall as if it were the hood of a car, and went to work. He removed the ruined lungs and replaced them with a lobe each from Phillips and Manglos. The surgery went perfectly. Not long after he awoke from the anesthesia, Matt asked for paper and pen and scrawled 30 exuberant pages of notes. "I'm so happy," he wrote. "I have been reborn."

Three years have passed, and Matt is three inches taller and 40 pounds heavier. He still has cystic fibrosis, and will have to battle to keep bacteria from infecting his new lungs. But the transplant has given him the precious gift of time (some recipients are still doing well ten years after the operation), during which he and everyone associated with CF hope a cure will be found. Matt often counsels other CF kids who are considering transplants, and saves up money from his job at Mitch's Surf Shop in La Jolla to make junkets to Fiji, Australia and Costa Rica. He spends time with his parents and grandparents, his brother and surfing pals, his girlfriend, Amelia. When asked what he gets upset about now, he says, "Only one thing: people who abuse their bodies."

He stays in touch with his donors too. On a warm San Diego night recently he could be found at a Moroccan restaurant, joking with Dave Manglos about whose drainage tubes had come out faster after the surgery (Matt's), who had complained more (a matter of debate), and whether his lung is having more fun now in Matt's body, traveling the world.

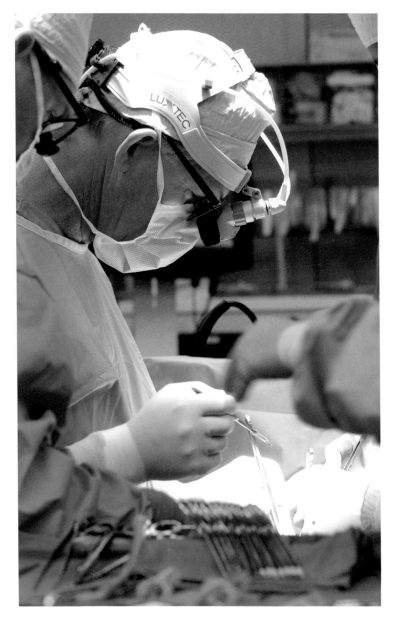

Dr. Vaughn Starnes, who pioneered the living donor lobar transplant, was the surgeon who performed the surgery on Matthew Joyce. **(Bob Riha, Jr./Childrens Hospital, Los Angeles/ Getty Images)**

The music is turned up. From the back room steps a belly dancer, who works her way among the tables clacking her finger cymbals and shaking her hips. As if prompted by some mysterious intuition, she stops next to Matt's seat, motioning for him to get up and dance with her. And he does, his body language surfer-cool, his face expressionless except for a tiny smile at the corners of his lips, a glint of gratitude, perhaps. Or just pure joy.

# The Ups and Downs of Cystic Fibrosis

**Grant**

The following article is written by Grant, a young adult with cystic fibrosis. Grant tells of the ups and downs of living with cystic fibrosis during his high school years. Always upbeat, he approached every-thing with a positive attitude, even having a feeding tube inserted in his stomach, or bringing an oxygen tank to school. Eventually, as his CF got progressively worse, Grant had to be home schooled. At sixteen he was told that he needed a lung transplant in order to sur-vive. Less than a month after having a double lung transplant, Grant was able to take part in his high school graduation. Grant got through his difficult times by having a positive attitude. Today he is a college student at the University of North Florida. Along with his mother, he created a nonprofit organization, called the Big Fun Foundation, that helps hospitalized kids alleviate stress and boredom.

I was diagnosed with cystic fibrosis (CF) when I was 7 months old. I am now 23. People with CF produce an abnormally thick mucus that clogs the respiratory

**SOURCE:** Kidshealth.org, "Cystic Fibrosis—Grant's Story," in Kidshealth.org, July 2008. Copyright © 1995–2008 The Nemours Foundation. Reproduced by permission.

FAST FACT

In 2005 only 2.6 percent of all lung transplant recipients were between the ages of eleven and seventeen, according to the U.S. Organ Procurement and Transplantation Network and the *Scientific Registry of Transplant Recipients 2006 Annual Report*.

and digestive systems. This congestion can lead to serious and frequent lung infections. Also, the body doesn't produce the natural enzymes needed for digestion of food and absorption of nutrients.

All these things can cause CF to take quite a toll on a person's energy level.

Luckily, I take enzymes by mouth so I can digest everything I eat. But I still had a very poor appetite as a kid and teen. I liked to eat; I just didn't eat much. So to get the right amount of calories per day, I had a feeding tube placed on top of my skin and attached to my stomach. Through this tube, I received a high-calorie, nutritional liquid during the night while I slept.

By the time I was 13, my cystic fibrosis was getting progressively worse. I got more and more lung infections and was in the hospital more often. I always fought back, recovered, and got back to my "normal" life. But eventually, the constant setbacks took their toll. My hospitalizations became more frequent, and I missed more days of school.

## Not Your Normal High-School Ups and Downs

Quite frankly, I was nervous about going into high school. Not only was I entering a new school and environment, I also knew my health was slowly getting worse. It was hard for me to do simple things, even carry books and walk to class. My teachers and I came up with ways to get around these problems—for example, I kept a book in each of my classrooms and one for every subject at home. And teachers would let me get out of class early to allow me time to walk to my next class.

One of the best things to do for CF is to get active. Physical activities such as basketball, tennis, or running

get the lungs working hard and can help clear extra mucus. Unfortunately, one of the last things I felt like doing in high school was running or playing a sport. Now that I exercise more and feel the benefits, I wish I had pushed myself to exercise more. It probably would have helped.

In the 9th grade I walked by the yearbook staffroom every day. They always looked like they were having fun. So in 10th grade, I applied to be on the staff and was accepted. It turned out to be the best thing for me during high school.

Everybody was so cool and had a great attitude toward my CF (mostly because I did, too). When I was having a "bad" day, they understood and gave me assistance if I needed it. The yearbook staff was my support group and just knowing they had my back helped me get through a lot of tough times.

It's wonderful to have friends around when you're feeling sick or even a little scared. I made incredible

One of the best things to do to help combat cystic fibrosis is regular physical activity, which helps loosen the mucus in the lungs. (© Sally and Richard Greenhill/ Alamy)

friends in school, often through getting involved in clubs, and I still keep in touch with many of them today. A few of them even told me they learned a lot from me about being positive and strong.

When I was 15, my doctor told me that I needed to take an oxygen tank around with me. This was pretty devastating; a sign that things were really getting bad. It was embarrassing having to wear the tubing around my nose all day and lug the tank around in my backpack.

In the beginning, I'd only wear it a little bit at school, mostly when I felt really short of breath. But I discovered that I needed it almost the entire time. My friends on the yearbook staff always offered to pay me for a couple of sniffs! I should have taken them up on that!

After a while, the oxygen became a part of me and I hardly noticed that I had it on most of the time (except when it irritated my upper lip)! It took a while, but I came to the realization that the oxygen wasn't an option, but a requirement. After I came to terms with it, I realized how much it helped me.

By my junior year, my CF was getting pretty bad and my stamina was even worse. My doctors recommended that I only stay at school for half a day and do my other subjects through home schooling. I was pretty psyched to get to leave school early every day, but found I missed out on a lot. It gave me more time to rest, eat, and do all of my CF treatments. But I missed my time with my friends.

By the time I was a senior, I was told I needed to stay home from school and do home-schooling every day. This bummed me out. Your senior year is supposed to be your best year in your entire school career. I was going to be home for mine. But I really had no choice. I just didn't have the stamina to go to school. I missed out on yearbook, dating, homecoming, prom, and all the other senior-year fun. I had to concentrate on taking care of myself as best I could.

# A Double-Lung Transplant

When I was 16, I was told that I would need a double-lung transplant if I wanted to survive. It would be a huge operation. But I knew that I wanted it because I wasn't done living. I had more to do and this was going to give me the power to do it.

In July 1998, I went to be evaluated to see if I'd be a good candidate for the transplant. I had to go through 2 days of medical tests, most of them exhausting. They included blood tests, X-rays, lung tests, scans, and even a psychiatric exam (to make sure I could handle the transplant emotionally).

That October, I was accepted as a candidate for the double-lung transplant. I was given a beeper so they could contact me and I could get to the hospital quickly if lungs became available for me. Unfortunately, my wait went on for almost 2 years. I had to take care of myself during this time because the better condition I was in for surgery, the better the outcome would be.

One night in May 2000, we got the call to come to the hospital. I was in surgery shortly after midnight. I woke up 8 hours later and my long recovery began. A combination of physical therapy, following doctor's directions, a good diet, emotional support, and determination helped me recover in about 1 1/2 months.

After my transplant, my doctors wanted me to get up out of bed as soon as possible to speed my recovery. My dad urged me to take short walks around the hospital a few times a day. I didn't want to because it hurt when I walked. But I took his advice and it helped me recover. Soon I was walking faster than him! I came back home on May 30 (25 days after surgery) to walk, without oxygen or assistance, in my high school graduation.

I still have cystic fibrosis, but now it's only in my digestive system. The transplant gave me lungs that do not have CF and never will. After the lung transplant, I was able to take long, deep breaths and had tons more energy and stamina. My appetite went from hardly eating to eating everything. My body needed more fuel now that it was running on all cylinders! My feeding tube was removed about a year after my transplant. I was really glad about that!

## Living—Really Living

It's been more than 5 years since my double-lung transplant and I have accomplished so much. I started college at the University of North Florida in January 2005. I am majoring in marketing and am working for my family's nonprofit foundation, The Big Fun Foundation.

I work out 5–6 times a week at the gym on campus. There is a wide range of exercise equipment, so I vary what I do every day for maximum benefit. I ran in my first 5K race in early December. When I was on oxygen and practically bedridden as a teenager, I never would have imagined I would be so active! The mix of cardio and weight training has, I believe, contributed to my good health nowadays.

I am responsible for 95% of my care now. There's a lot to do! I still take medications—in fact I take more pills now (about 30 a day!) than I had to take before my transplant. Keeping up with numerous appointments, taking my medicines on time, and being on the lookout for any changes in the way I feel make for a busy schedule in addition to my classes. But taking charge of myself gives me a sense of pride when I see how far I've come after 23 years of ups and downs with cystic fibrosis.

Sure, I've had some setbacks, including a couple of hospitalizations. But I apply the same attitude I always have: Think positive, do what's needed to get better, and move on.

# A Mother's Story

**Margaret Simmons**

In the following article Margaret Simmons provides a parent's perspective of cystic fibrosis. Margaret's daughter Laura was born with cystic fibrosis in 1991. Margaret says that as a baby, Laura was constantly sick and always taking antibiotics. Margaret knew something was wrong with her daughter, but doctors kept telling her that Laura was fine. Finally, just before Laura's third birthday, Margaret and her husband found out their daughter had cystic fibrosis. As Margaret learned more about the disease she became heartbroken. Her daughter had a severe form of the CF gene and her life expectancy was only five years. For a time, Margaret and her husband prepared and planned for Laura's death. Then eventually, Margaret let go of her fears of death and put her daughter's life in God's hands. When Margaret wrote this (2007), Laura was a happy and active sixteen-year-old.

The best place to start would be explaining why I chose this topic, Cystic Fibrosis. My oldest daughter Laura has Cystic Fibrosis (CF). I'm not fond of

**SOURCE:** Margaret Simmons, "Handing Over My Faith to God, a Mother's Story," in YourHub.com (West Niagra County), April 15, 2007. Copyright © 2007 The Buffalo News. Reproduced by permission.

saying she "has it," it isn't like "it" can be given back, although I wish it could be. I'm going to give you a mother's perspective of our journey with Laura and her CF.

## She Was Always Sick

From about my first trimester of pregnancy something came up on one of my routine tests and I went to get an Alpha-Feto Protein (AFP) test. This test typically screens for Down syndrome and Spina Bifida not for CF. I recall that phone call from Women's and Children's Hospital of Buffalo (WCHOB). They told me that there wasn't anything wrong and if I wanted to know what I was going to have. I agreed and they told me that I was going to have a healthy baby girl! Never thought twice about my daughter's outcomes in life (health wise).

Laura was born without any problems except that she was a little jaundiced. Ok, I could deal with that. I breastfed her and went back to the hospital daily until her jaundice was gone. On our last visit to the hospital to be tested the technician stated that she looked like she was stuffy or sick. Like many new moms I promptly took her to the doctor. This is when her symptoms of CF started to appear. Her Doctor told me she was fine and not to be worried. She had a minor sinus infection. Please keep in mind she was only less than two weeks old and already had her first sinus infection. At this point I didn't know that chronic sinusitis was a symptom of CF. Laura's life went on this way for a long time; on an antibiotic off an antibiotic. Sometimes the antibiotic treatment was for a typical 10 days, others were for month long treatments. I kept asking my doctor if this was normal, he told me yes, sometimes kids are sick, but for this long? Laura was getting closer to her second birthday and she had in this short amount of time had one operation to have adenoids removed, flat lined from an allergic reaction to an antibiotic, and had only gone about a total of three months without an antibiotic! My daughter had almost died and

I was about at my wit's end. I began to demand answers. I switched doctors and went to what some called Lockport's (upstate New York) best pediatrician. There I was treated like a neurotic parent and every time my daughter had loose stools or a runny nose I called and made an appointment. Again no one ever told me that these were symptoms of CF. Yet again, I was told she was fine. She was taller than 100% of her age group and at the correct weight for that height.

The leading doctor handed me a script and said "To make you happy I'll have her tested, although I know there is nothing wrong with her." Off to WCHOB Laura and I went. It was snowing and right before her third birthday. I remember being hopeful and confused. Laura's speech was impaired by now because of all of her ear and sinus infections. I remember registering, Laura was so happy to be there. "Hi! I'm Wrawa Cinnamons." The registration person looked up at me, I corrected "Laura Simmons." After that happy moment, life as we knew it, began to quickly change forever.

Laura skipped over to the elevator and pushed the up button. We got on and went to the third floor, there we were greeted by a nice woman named Margaret Harris. Margaret does all of the sweat testing for possible CF patients. Margaret explained that this was a painless test and that it only takes three simple steps. 1.Stimulation of the sweat glands. 2. Collection of the gauze. 3. Analysis. We were able to drive back home after the second step. Laura was happy she had a toy and a sticker. I was worried and no sticker for me. I remember the phone call. My husband called me at my grandmother's house: "What is CF? Why does that hospital want you to come back?" I didn't have any answers for him. I went straight to the doctor's office and waited in the lobby, it was full of parents and their children. The doctor came out and called for his next patient. I said I was next. I was demanding right there in front of everyone what was CF!

"Make an appointment and we can talk about it later." I didn't think so. I got my way and we "talked".

## Finding Out About Cystic Fibrosis

This is when I found out what those two letters "C-F" meant. I found out that CF is an inherited disease that causes thick, sticky mucus to build up in the lungs and digestive tract. It is the most common type of chronic lung disease in children and young adults, and may result in early death. I was in shock and madder than I care to admit. I just looked at the doctor and told him, "I'm so glad that this test made me so happy! My daughter is going to die and you said she was fine!"

This next trip to WGHOB was filled with terror and tears. Laura was happy she was going to go back and hoping she would get another toy. You know you are in for some seriously bad news when you enter a large conference room and there is coffee and food on the table and around that table is the whole CF Lung center team. A very nice nurse took Laura happily away to finish her testing. (Laura is the type of child that would walk away with anyone.) My husband and I entered the room to meet our new "extended family." There we were told what was going to happen next and for the rest of her life.

Our first question was who gave CF to her. That is when we found out both parents have to be at least carriers of the defective gene. Millions of Americans carry the CF gene, but show no symptoms of CF. Our second question was how long did she have left to live. At our first meeting they couldn't tell us that until the complete DNA analysis was done. We found out one long month later that her defective gene was severe and that her life would most likely end somewhere around five years old. Later we found out that there are over 1,000 mutations of the CF gene and she had one of the rare ones.

Later that day we met up with Laura again; she was loaded with tons of stickers and a few more toys. Holding back the tears I gave her a hug and that is when she said she had something called "roses." I asked the social worker what was Laura talking about and she told me about the story of "65 Roses." Mary G. Weiss a mother much like myself back in 1965 was talking on the phone trying to raise money for the newly formed CF foundation and her son Richard overheard her talking and told his mom what she was working for. He said, " You are working for 65 Roses." That name sounded softer to me than CF. I also found out this is how they teach young children like Laura how to say Cystic Fibrosis—65 Roses.

An unfortunate reality for parents is that when they focus on their child with cystic fibrosis, they must also factor in the child's possible death from the disease. (AP Images)

We learned so much that month after being told she had CF. We found out that we had to give her a high fat and calorie diet, because her pancreas was shutting down and she needed the extra nutrition. Now it has been

reported that there may be a link to her type of diet and improved lung function. The report stated that the CF patient needs 120–150% of recommended daily energy allowance. By the time Laura was 4 she was taking almost 10 pills a meal to help digest her food. Testing showed that her pancreas was almost nonfunctional.

## Focusing on Life, Not Death

Laura used to say she loved her "roses" because mommy beats her back and it feels so good! We had to do Chest PT [physiotherapy] on her 2–3 times a day to help move the mucus out of her lungs. We gave her her inhaler and sometimes her extra "new" test meds. As she got closer to her fifth birthday we got prepared for her death not her birthday. We were told that not much else could be done; just keep making her happy and comfortable. Yes, we have a grave already paid for and what we want to have done when she dies. Seems strange today to be saying that. After her party, I cried and prayed for a long time. Then and there I slowly handed my faith over to God. Then I started to live like she was living and gave up on the idea that she was going to die. Trust me that was a long battle in itself. We have gone to WCHOB so many times now; my car can get there almost on autopilot.

Laura was granted a "Wish" and we went to Disney World when she was seven. It was a wonderful time. Laura rode in a wheel chair most of the time because of the heat. CF patients sweat much more than you or I and become dehydrated faster also. We had to be extra careful of other people's germs and keep a high level of infection control. Disney accommodated us very well. They made sure that we never waited in line too long and cleaned the handles of the rides before Laura got on them. I was amazed! The smiles I saw will always warm my heart forever!

For a long time I told Laura no you can't play there or you can't do this. Then I thought about her quality of life, was I giving her a fair chance like other kids? So I handed my child and 100% of my faith to God. He knows best! I slowly let her go and do and play. I let her grow up! "HE" let her grow up!

Laura is amazing! Her sister is also. Ann Marie is just a carrier of CF. We had her tested also. My daughters are wonderful and match each other well. When Laura is sick Ann is right there taking care of her or maybe even hounding Laura to take her meds. God has given me these wonderful girls to help tell everyone about CF.

## What a Miracle She Is

I could go on and on with our story about Laura so in my summary I want to tell you just some of the things a sick kid with CF that should be dead today has accomplished in her 16 years of life so far. Did you catch that she is 16? She has been through many "mid-life crises"(if you think about it the median age keeps going up so she keeps having mid-life crises) her first was at 2 1/2 and we didn't even know it, we just thought it was the terrible two's. She has climbed a mountain in the Adirondacks. She has given back to her community with over 1,100 community hours! The president of the United States has given her two golden awards for her efforts. She swims long distance competitively on the JV [junior varsity] squad. She has danced, sang, and even tried hockey! She walks in the yearly Great Strides for CF walk and this year [2007] she is on the funding committee. Laura touches lives! She is here with a purpose, to tell everyone that has a child with CF, "Yes we can, just watch us grow!" Laura is a miracle, she even awes the doctors with the achievements she has done. They just shake their heads and smile.

> **FAST FACT**
>
> In 2006 the predicted median age of survival for those with cystic fibrosis was thirty-seven years.

# GLOSSARY

**acetylcysteine** An antioxidant drug used to reduce the thickness of mucus and ease its removal.

**amniocentesis** Procedure used in prenatal diagnosis to obtain amniotic fluid which can be used for genetic and other diagnostic tests.

**biofilm** A substance that sticks to wet surfaces. Biofilms can form on solid or liquid surfaces as well as on soft tissue in living organisms. They are usually difficult to dissolve. In cystic fibrosis, a biofilm is formed by *Pseudomonas aeruginosa* bacteria and prevents antibiotics from killing the bacteria.

**bronchiectasis** Permanent dilatation (widening) of the bronchi (the large air tubes which begin at the bottom of the trachea and branch into the lungs). Bronchiectasis can result in very serious illness including recurrent respiratory infections, a disabling cough, shortness of breath, and hemoptysis (coughing up blood).

***Burkholderia cepacia*** A pathogenic bacterium that infects the lungs of cystic fibrosis patients. The bacterium is resistant to antibiotics and easily spread between people with CF. This bacterium can cause life-threatening lung infections.

**cadaveric** Having to do with a dead body (a cadaver).

**carrier** A person with one copy of a defective gene, who does not have the disease it causes, but can pass along the defective gene to offspring.

**cystic fibrosis–related diabetes (CFRD)** A unique type of diabetes that afflicts cystic fibrosis sufferers. It shares features of types 1 and 2 diabetes, but it is a unique and distinct form.

| | |
|---|---|
| **cystic fibrosis transmembrane conductance regulator (CFTR)** | The protein responsible for regulating chloride movement across cells in some tissues. |
| **cystic fibrosis transmembrane conductance regulator (CFTR) gene** | The gene responsible for making a defective CFTR protein. When a person has two defective copies of the CFTR gene, cystic fibrosis is the result. |
| **delta F508 (ΔF508)** | The most common genetic mutation of the cystic fibrosis transmembrane conductance regulator (CFTR) gene. In this mutation, the CFTR gene is missing the amino acid phenylalanine at position #508. |
| **diabetes** | When used alone, the term diabetes refers to diabetes mellitus, which is a syndrome characterized by abnormally high levels of sugar in the blood. There are two types of diabetes mellitus, type 1 and type 2. In people with type 1 diabetes, the pancreas is unable to make insulin. Type 2 diabetes is caused by the body's lack of response to insulin produced by the pancreas, sometimes called insulin resistance. |
| **double lung transplant** | Double lung transplants involve an incision below the breasts and take about six to twelve hours of surgery. Both lungs are replaced. |
| **enzymes** | Proteins that act as catalysts in mediating and speeding a specific chemical reaction. |
| **gene** | The basic biological unit of heredity made of deoxyribonucleic acid (DNA). |
| **genetic testing** | Tests that identify certain genes or parts of genes for the purpose of diagnosing a genetic disease in children and adults; identifying future disease risks; or identifying the risks of disease for future children. |

| | |
|---|---|
| **living donor lung transplant** | A lung transplant procedure where very ill patients who cannot wait for cadaveric lungs obtain lung segments, or lobes, from two different living donors. |
| **meconium ileus** | One of the first symptoms of cystic fibrosis. The meconium, which is the first stool of an infant, becomes thickened and congested in the ileum of the small intestine. |
| **mucolytic** | An agent that dissolves or destroys mucin, the chief component of mucus. |
| **mucoviscidosis** | An older name for cystic fibrosis, used more commonly in Europe. |
| **pancreas** | A digestive organ about six inches long that stretches across the back of the abdomen, behind the stomach. The pancreas secretes digestive enzymes and hormones, such as insulin. |
| **pancreatic insufficiency** | Reduction or absence of pancreatic secretions into the digestive system due to scarring and blockage of the pancreatic duct. |
| **pathogenic bacteria** | Infectious bacteria that cause disease. |
| ***Pseudomonas aeruginosa*** | The most common pathogenic bacterium infecting the lungs of cystic fibrosis sufferers. |
| **recessive gene** | Genes are either dominant or recessive. A dominant gene's characteristics will predominate when paired with a recessive gene. For a recessive gene to show, it must be paired with another recessive gene. |
| ***Staphylococcus aureus*** | A pathogenic bacteria that often causes infections in the lungs of cystic fibrosis sufferers. |
| **sweat** | A colorless transparent acidic fluid with a distinctive odor secreted by the small tubular sudoriferous (sweat) glands situated within the skin and under it in the subcutaneous tissue. |
| **sweat test** | A simple test that measures the amount of sodium chloride (salt) in sweat and is used to diagnose cystic fibrosis. |

# CHRONOLOGY

| B.C. | 544–255 | Radiocarbon dating of human bones indicates that cystic fibrosis was present among the Iron Age population. |
|------|---------|-------------|
| A.D. | 1500 | In medieval folklore, infants with salty skin, a symptom of cystic fibrosis, are considered "bewitched" because they routinely die an early death. |
| | 1905 | Karl Landsteiner describes meconium ileus. |
| | 1936 | Swiss physician Guido Fanconi publishes a report describing children with "cystic pancreas fibromatosis and bronchiectasis." |
| | 1938 | After performing autopsies on infants and children, Dorothy Andersen, of Columbia University in New York, provides the first comprehensive description of the symptoms of cystic fibrosis and of the changes produced in organs. Andersen's paper, "Cystic Fibrosis of the Pancreas and its Relation to Celiac Disease: A Clinical and Pathological Study," was the first report that clearly defined CF as a distinct disease. |
| | 1946 | Dorothy Andersen and her colleague R.G. Hodges hypothesize that CF is a recessive inherited disease. |
| | 1950s | Few children with cystic fibrosis live to attend elementary school. |

**1953**    Based on his observations during a New York City heat wave, physician Paul di Sant'Agnese recognizes that children with cystic fibrosis have an increased amount of salt in their sweat. His observations lead to the development of the sweat test.

**1955**    The National Cystic Fibrosis Research Foundation (later to become the Cystic Fibrosis Foundation) is formed.

**1960**    About 4 percent of children born with CF live beyond their teens.

**1963**    James Hardy performs the first human lung transplant on a patient with lung cancer. The patient survives for eighteen days.

**1965**    The International Cystic Fibrosis (Mucoviscidosis) Foundation is formed in Paris.

**Early 1980s**    Researchers link the organ damage caused by CF with a malfunction of the epithelial tissue. Paul Quinton of the University of California finds that chloride intake is impaired in the sweat glands, and Michael Knowles and Richard Boucher of the University of North Carolina find that chloride transport in lung epithelial tissue is deficient.

**1983**    At Presbyterian-University Hospital in Pittsburgh, a twenty-five-year-old man from East Aurora, New York, is the first cystic fibrosis patient to receive a heart-lung transplant. He is operated on by Bartley Griffith.

**1988**    A twenty-nine-year-old British Columbia man is the first cystic fibrosis patient to undergo a successful double lung transplant. He is operated on at Toronto General Hospital by Joel Cooper.

**1989**   Teams led by Lap-Chee Tsui and Jack Riordan at the Hospital for Sick Children in Toronto, Ontario, and Francis S. Collins at the University of Michigan identify the cystic fibrosis transmembrane conductance regulator (CFTR) gene on human chromosome 7.

**1993**   The first experimental gene therapy treatment is given to a cystic fibrosis patient.

**2000**   Scientists map the entire genetic sequence of the most common cause of CF lung infections—the *Pseudomonas aeruginosa* bacterium.

**2006**   The median predicted survival age for cystic fibrosis patients is 36.9 years.

# ORGANIZATIONS TO CONTACT

**Boomer Esiason Foundation**
52 Vanderbilt Ave.
15th Fl.
New York, NY 10017
(646) 292-7930
fax: (646) 292-7945
http://esiason.org

The Boomer Esiason Foundation was founded by the former football player after his son Gunnar was diagnosed with cystic fibrosis in 1993. The foundation raises money for research aimed at finding a cure for cystic fibrosis and works to educate the public about the disease. The foundation publishes a monthly newsletter, the *BEF Update*.

**Canadian Cystic Fibrosis Foundation**
2221 Yonge St.
Ste. 601
Toronto, Ontario,
M4S 2B4
(416) 485-9149
fax: (416) 485-0960
www.cysticfibrosis.ca

The mission of the Canadian Cystic Fibrosis Foundation is to help people with cystic fibrosis (CF). The foundation does this by funding research toward the goal of a cure or control for CF, supporting high quality CF care, promoting public awareness of CF, and raising funds for these purposes. The Canadian CF Foundation publishes various brochures, newsletters, and reports.

**Cystic Fibrosis Foundation (CFF)**
6931 Arlington Rd.
Bethesda, MD 20814
(301) 951-4422
fax: (301) 951-6378
www.cff.org

CFF is a nonprofit organization committed to finding a cure for cystic fibrosis and to improving the quality of life for those with the disease. The foundation funds and accredits CF care centers and adult care programs and sponsors various fund-raising events, such as *Great Strides* walks. The CFF publishes *Commitment*, an electronic newsletter, and the annual *CF Patient Registry*, which provides statistics and demographics about CF patients in the United States.

**Cystic Fibrosis Research Inc. (CFRI)**
Bayside Business Plaza
2672 Bayshore Pkwy
Ste. 520
Mountain View, CA
94043
(650) 404-9975
fax: (650) 404-9981
www.cfri.org/home
.html

CFRI is a nonprofit volunteer organization dedicated to attaining the highest quality of life for children and adults who have cystic fibrosis. The organization sponsors CF research and provides educational programs and personal support. Three times a year, CFRI publishes *CFRI News*, a newsletter about the latest in CF research developments and other topics of interest to members of the CF community.

**Cystic Fibrosis Worldwide (CFW)**
Executive Director
Ms. Christine Noke
210 Park Ave. #267
Worcester, MA 01609
(508) 733-6120
www.cfww.org

CFW is an international nonprofit organization that works to ensure that all people worldwide who suffer from cystic fibrosis are educated about the disease and have access to appropriate care. CFW also works to improve the knowledge of CF among medical professionals and governments worldwide. Activities of CFW include providing an international platform for the exchange of knowledge and supporting a cure for cystic fibrosis. The *CFW Newsletter* provides information about cystic fibrosis on an international level.

**March of Dimes Birth Defects Foundation**
1275 Mamaroneck Ave.
White Plains, NY
10605
(914) 428-7100
fax: (914) 428-8203
www.marchofdimes
.com

The March of Dimes is one of the oldest U.S. organizations devoted to improving the health of babies. The March of Dimes raises money to help prevent birth defects, genetic disorders, premature births, and infant deaths. The March of Dimes carries out its mission through research, community service, education, and advocacy. The organization publishes a monthly email newsletter called *Miracles.*

**National Heart, Lung and Blood Institute (NHLBI)**
Bldg. 31,
Rm. 5A48
31 Center Dr.
MSC 2486
Bethesda, MD 20892
(301) 592-8573
fax: (240) 629-3246
www.nhlbi.nih.gov

THE NHLBI, a member of the National Institutes of Health, is the lead U.S. governmental health agency that deals with diseases of the heart, blood vessels, lungs, and blood. The NHLBI plans and directs research in development and evaluation of interventions and devices related to prevention, treatment, and rehabilitation of patients suffering from heart, lung, and blood diseases and disorders. The NHLBI publication Web site provides innumerable publications about heart, lung, and blood diseases.

**National Human Genome Research Institute (NHGRI)**
Communications and Public Liaison Branch
National Human Genome Research Institute
National Institutes of Health
Bldg. 31,
Rm. 4B09
31 Center Dr.,
MSC 2152
9000 Rockville Pike
Bethesda, MD 20892-2152
(301) 402-0911
fax: (301) 402-2218
www.genome.gov

The NHGRI is a member of the National Institutes of Health (NIH) and the nation's lead federal agency concerned with the study of genetic diseases. The institute led the Human Genome Project for the NIH which in 2003 mapped the entire human genome. The NHGRI supports the development of resources and technology that will accelerate genome research and its application to human health. The NHGRI provides many educational and informational resources, including *DNA Day Previews*, a monthly newsletter, and *50 Years of DNA: A Celebration of the Genome*.

**United States Adults Cystic Fibrosis Association, Inc. (USACFA)**
PO Box 1618
Gresham, OR
97030-0519
(503) 669-3561
fax: (503) 669-3561
www.cfroundtable
.com

USACFA was formed in 1990 as an independent nonprofit organization operated entirely by adult volunteers who have cystic fibrosis. The purpose of USACFA is to provide a source of information for CF adults regarding the basis, nature, and progression of the disease, as well as the latest treatments and research to fight it, and to provide a forum for CF adults to communicate with each other. The organization publishes a quarterly newsletter called *CF Roundtable*.

# FOR FURTHER READING

## Books

Andrew Bush, ed., *Cystic Fibrosis in the 21st Century*. New York: Karger, 2006.

Isabel Stenzel Byrnes and Anabel Stenzel, *The Power of Two: A Twin Triumph over Cystic Fibrosis*. Columbia: University of Missouri Press, 2007.

Heather Summerhayes Cariou, *Sixtyfive Roses: A Sister's Memoir*. Toronto: McArthur, 2007.

Margaret Hodson, Duncan Geddes, and Andrew Bush, *Cystic Fibrosis*. New York: Hodder Arnold, 2007.

A. Kalfoglou et al., *Reproductive Genetic Testing: What America Thinks*. Washington, DC: Genetics and Public Policy Center, 2004.

Teresa Anne Mullin, *The Stones Applaud: How Cystic Fibrosis Shaped My Childhood*. Franklin, TN: Providence House, 2007.

David Orenstein, *Cystic Fibrosis: A Guide for Patient and Family*. Philadelphia: Lippincott, Williams & Wilkins, 2003.

Frank Harold Stephenson, *DNA: How the Biotech Revolution Is Changing the Way We Fight Disease*. Amherst, NY: Prometheus, 2007.

Keith Wailoo and Stephen Pemberton, *The Troubled Dream of Genetic Medicine*. Baltimore: Johns Hopkins University Press, 2006.

## Periodicals

Shaw D. Aaron, "*Pseudomonas aeruginosa* and Cystic Fibrosis —a Nasty Bug Gets Nastier," *Respiration*, 2006.

Philip M. Farrell, "The Meaning of 'Early' Diagnosis in a New Era of Cystic Fibrosis Care," *Pediatrics*, January 2007.

Jennifer Gish, "Mother and Daughter Battle Cystic Fibrosis Together," *Albany (NY) Times Union*, March 14, 2006.

Dana Goldstein, "Genetic Disorder," *In These Times,* July 6, 2007. www.inthesetimes.com/article/3231/genetic_disorder.

Sam Jaffe, "Can Two Killers Make a Cure?" *New Scientist,* June 11, 2005.

Carlos E. Milla, Joanne Billings, and Antoinette Moran, "Diabetes Is Associated with Dramatically Decreased Survival in Female but Not Male Subjects with Cystic Fibrosis," *Diabetes Care,* September 2005.

Don Monroe, "Looking for Chinks in the Armor of Bacterial Biofilms," *PLoS Biology,* November 2007. www.pubmed central .nih.gov/articlerender.fcgi?artid=2071939.

Ann Parks, "Wrongful Birth: Question of Choice," *Baltimore Daily Record,* July 25, 2006.

Peggy Peck, "Studies Look to Sea for Cystic Fibrosis Treatment," *MedPageToday.com,* January 19, 2006. www.medpage today. com/InfectiousDisease/URItheFlu/tb/2510.

Richard W. Sams, "Faces Disappearing: The Implications of Cystic Fibrosis Screening," *New Atlantis,* Summer 2007.

Bonnie Schindler, "Pregnant Questions: Prenatal Testing Offers Parents More Information—but Presents Agonizing Questions as Well," *Pittsburgh City Paper,* November 29, 2007. www.pitts burghcitypaper.ws/gyrobase/Content?oid=oid%3A38858.

Liz Szabo, "Maze of Cystic Fibrosis Is Getting a Little Clearer," *USA Today,* February 13, 2006.

Michael J. Welsh and Alan E. Smith, "Cystic Fibrosis," *Scientific American,* December 1995.

Stefan Worgall, "A Realistic Chance for Gene Therapy in the Near Future," *Pediatric Nephrology,* February 2005.

# INDEX